RESPECT

RESPECT

WOMEN

AND

POPULAR MUSIC

DOROTHY MARCIC

TEXERE

NEW YORK • LONDON

Published by

TEXERE
55 East 52nd Street
New York, NY 10055
www.etexere.com

Tel: +1 (212) 317 5106
Fax: +1 (212) 317 5178

In the UK:

TEXERE Publishing Limited
71–77 Leadenhall Street
London EC3A 3DE
www.etexere.co.uk

Tel: +44 (0)20 7204 3644
Fax: +44 (0)20 7208 6701

This publication is designed to provide accurate and authoritative information in regard to the subject matter covered. It is sold with the understanding that the publisher is not engaged in rendering legal, accounting, or other professional services. If legal advice or other expert assistance is required, the services of a competent professional person should be sought.

Designed by Elliott Beard

Library of Congress Cataloging in Publication Data has been applied for.

ISBN 1-58799-083-0

Printed in the United States of America.

This book is printed on acid-free paper.

10 9 8 7 6 5 4 3 2 1

To my grandmothers,
Dorothy Nelson Stordock and Josephine Druks Marcic,
who lived courageously through many hardships,
teaching me respect and strength.

CONTENTS

Contents

FOREWORD

*F*or centuries women have fought the internal, and often external, battle to find their rightful place in this world. Early in the last century, women were nothing more than property to be traded or owned. Any rights enjoyed as a single woman were often withdrawn when she married. Indeed, a woman gave up so many civil and property rights upon crossing the threshold that she was said to be entering a "civil death." Married women generally were not allowed to make contracts, devise wills, take part in other legal transactions, or control any wages they might earn. If the laws that had created such a chasm between men and women were ever to change, then women had to be heard in the halls of Congress. To do that, they would first need to gain the right to vote. And so, the movement began in which women fought for their right to vote and be treated as equals. They fought for their rightful place in the world with the written word and with song.

War has a way of changing the landscape of our world. It forces individuals to take on new roles that otherwise might not be allowed. In World War II, women worked in factories and flew planes from

London to the European continent for pilots to use. When the war was over and men returned to claim their positions as head of house and breadwinner, some women found giving up their freedom of choice a bitter pill to swallow.

In the early years of country music, songs often trended toward "cheating songs," with the blame falling on the woman who failed to take care of her man. In 1951, Hank Thompson released a song called "The Wild Side of Life" that spent fifteen weeks at number one. In the song, Thompson chides the woman who deserts his love for the glamour of nightlife. The distinctive chorus line, "I didn't know God made honky-tonk angels," would inspire a response that would make Kitty Wells a household name. After a failed 1949–50 stint at RCA Victor, Kitty was about to quit showbiz and stay at home with her three children when Paul Cohen at Decca Records asked her husband, Johnny Wright, if Kitty would be interested in recording the answer to Hank Thompson's number-one song. She agreed and in 1952, Kitty Wells released "It Wasn't God Who Made Honky-Tonk Angels" as a response to Hank Thompson's "The Wild Side of Life." In the words of Kitty's song, she put the blame on the man who failed to appreciate the woman and treat her right. It "wasn't God who made honky-tonk angels" but the man at home who drove her to it. Those were strong words coming from a woman. Although the Grand Ole Opry banned the song and she wasn't allowed to perform it on the air at the time, the massive hit swept the nation and transformed the mother of three and the wife of Johnny Wright into the Queen of Country Music. The song was a million-selling record, reaching the coveted number-one slot on the chart—the first time that had ever been accomplished by a female artist. A few years later, Loretta Lynn would be a rabble-rouser in the country format by releasing songs like "The Pill" and "Don't Come Home a Drinkin' (With Lovin' on Your Mind)." "The Pill" was also banned from the airwaves of many radio stations, but women flocked to the stores and bought the anthem of their time. Women began to write and sing what they felt as a release from the restrictions society had placed on them. As women began to feel an alliance with one another, they became stronger. A few stepped out to change the world through song.

In the music industry, women have fought the battle to be heard in song and behind the scenes in executive offices throughout the United States. When I got my first job in the Nashville music industry in 1976, most women didn't have last names. At least, if they had them, they didn't use them. My first job was receptionist at Monument Records. I noticed right away that women would call the office and ask for someone and use only their first name and the company they represented. When men would call, they would always identify themselves with their full name and company name. That was my first lesson and one I have passed along many times to employees I have had down through the years.

Today's corporations tell you they strive for equality in the workplace. They provide diversity training and insist they protect against discrimination, sexism, and harassment. But corporate personnel offices are often thousands of miles away from the day-to-day office routines where these actions take place. The music industry—both for artists and for the employees behind the scenes—is often very different from the external perception of those looking in. If you want to succeed in business, you don't talk about these things—even today.

Women today struggle with the same issues their mothers did. If we become successful executives, we must balance that role with family responsibilities. Regardless of our newfound quality, the creation of home and hearth primarily falls to the woman. In business we strive to be the best we can be while still being the best wife, mother, and homemaker. We are the tough close-the-deal business executive at work. Then we walk out that door and strive to serve our husbands and our children when we leave work and begin our second job at home.

Down through history, women have found their release through song. From the Negro spirituals who sang about "sweet chariots bending down to lift us up" to Lee Ann Womack singing a message of hope to future generations of living life to its fullest with "I Hope You Dance," women have poured out their hearts in song. We ask, "Who am I?" "What importance do I have?" "Can anyone hear what I am saying?" Dr. Marcic heard those voices and chronicled the history of these songs in the twentieth century.

SHELIA SHIPLEY BIDDY
President and owner,
Shipley Biddy Entertainment
Former senior vice president and
general manager for Decca Records
(1994–1999)

INTRODUCTION

For more than the first half of the twentieth century, the voice of women in Top 40 popular music has been one of neediness and dependency. Please love me; I'll do anything for you; just be my baby, even if you're no good and treat me bad; hey, I'll even do the cooking and pay the rent—just *love* me and I'll stand by my man. But if you leave me, well, it will be the end of the world.

By the end of the century, things sounded different. Popular music had women looking for the hero within themselves, wanting a man to stand beside rather than in front of them, being urged to get on their feet and make it happen, ready to stand on their own with or without a man. The road from one to the other wasn't easy or straight.

Women's voices in Top 40 hits moved from dependency to sexpot, starting in the 1930s with the Betty Boop phenomenon. During World War II there was a short reprieve from doormat status when men went off to war and Rosie the Riveter took over—and a women's minor-league baseball association was established. Music of women had some strength, but that quickly faded when the war ended. Men came home and the women went back into the home. From the 1950s through the mid-1960s, the message was one of rigid gender roles (oh how she enjoys being a girl), focus on materialism (diamonds are a girl's best friend, after all)and more wishing and hoping and praying that he will just love her.

Then it changed. The publication of Betty Friedan's *The Feminine Mystique* and the protest movements created a new consciousness. The tune moved from total dependency to a sense of unease; something felt not right. She was still powerless in his presence, but she was beginning to see her deal was not so great. Sure, he was a sweet-talking guy and not to be trusted, but he was her kind of guy. About the same time that affirmative action and the Equal Employment Opportunity Commission (EEOC) became law, our women singers started to push back with anger, saying "you don't own me" or all she wants is a little R-E-S-P-E-C-T, which turned to revenge and the promise of how her boots were gonna walk all over him.

There was a growing consciousness. The songs sung by women showed a new awareness of just how wronged she had been all these years. By the seventies, she was ready to show her own strength, just as Billie Jean King did in 1973 when she beat Bobby Riggs in the "Battle of the Sexes" tennis match. That new strength was reflected in song, too. Initially, it was power born of anger. Helen Reddy's "I Am Woman" or Gloria Gaynor's "I Will Survive." But even the recognition of anger was too much to bear, and the 1980s brought a rash of cynical songs. Gushy hopes were gone as the nation finally recognized a new syndrome. In 1985, Connecticut's Tracey Thurman became the first woman to win a civil suit as a battered wife. Similarly, Madonna and Tina Turner were not singing about mushy love or even anger, but rather of hopelessness about the pipe dreams they had lived. They belted out messages of what's love got to do with it, and how the material girl of today doesn't care for love but wants only cold, hard cash.

Inner strength appeared in the nineties. Oprah became the highest-paid entertainer in 1993 at $49 million per year, the very same year Mariah Carey's number-one song crooned advice to find the hero within. At the end of the decade, Jo Dee Messina wanted a man who would stand beside her, not in front; Shania Twain was clear about wanting him to love *her*, no matter what; and the Dixie Chicks crooned about the modern young girl's hopes and opportunities out in wide-open spaces. It was the first time that women stood on their own, without leaning on a man or pushing back against him. Not coincidentally, it was the first time that women's popular music was finally selling like that of male singers. The new era had arrived.

This book will share the journey of women in popular music throughout the twentieth century. The songs are those that tell a story about women—their roles and their needs—and those that spoke to me. These are not the sentimental love songs but rather the songs about how women were seen as women—by themselves or others.

ARCHETYPES

One reason the charted songs *were* so successful is that they touched a deep nerve in the culture and represented an archetype of women for that era. Psychologist Carl Jung first coined the term *archetype* to indicate some psychological predisposition toward certain patterns which create a blueprint in our psyches. For example, one of Jung's archetypes was that of the *Warrior* (for example, Wonder Woman, as shown in the table on page xvii). Every culture has heroes that map onto the Warrior archetype. It might be a brave soldier, or it might be some courageous person who defied injustice. Examples of heroes as the Warrior include David (of David and Goliath), Xena: Warrior Princess, Superman, Sir Thomas More (who lost his life for challenging King Henry VIII's repeal of the Vatican's divorce law), and 1930s aviatrix Amelia Earhart, the first woman to fly solo over the Atlantic.

Similarly, I believe the charted hits became popular because many of them hooked into common archetypes. As our culture developed and the education and opportunities of women became enhanced, those archetypes changed. In the first sixty or so years of the twentieth century, women's voice in popular music was mostly that of dependence and compliance, much like that of a child. The progression of women's voice in popular music moves from the compliant child to rebel teenager to young adult cynic to, finally, mature and responsible adult. On the opposite page is a chart that shows the progression of the archetypes in popular music, along with one or two icons that represent each archetype.

Another way to analyze these stages is through archetypal themes. All of the songs can be fitted into one of these four groups: love, war, aspiration, and wisdom. Merging these two models together shows that the love theme was the predominant one in the first half of the century, though it continued as well throughout the time period. War as a theme emerged in the teenage rebellious stage, while aspiration emerged in the midst of the rebellious and young adult cynical stages. It was at this time that love was not expected to solve all problems, so there was a need to have other hopes. Finally, wisdom showed itself in the adult phase, with the introduction of a series of songs on personal growth and spiritual development.

Dependency and compliance is the message from 1900 through 1929. Betty Boop and Harriet Nelson (of the TV show *Ozzie and Harriet*) typify those norms, while Janis Joplin is the consummate rebellious teenager featured in the 1960s. As the real truth about love was seen, we moved into the cynical young adult phase in the 1970s. Who to better represent that than Princess Diana, who showed the world how futile were the Prince Charming and happily-ever-after myths? Tina Turner epitomized those feelings in "What's Love Got to Do with It?" Finally, in the 1990s women come into their own inner strength in popular music, the new archetype is one of Lilith as mature adult, exemplified by Oprah Winfrey, today's modern heroine. Lilith was the first wife of Adam, the first man in the Bible. Lilith left the Garden of Eden after she refused to be subservient, a Compliant. Adam ordered her to obey and she refused, saying they were equal. Although there are many examples of mature, independent and successful women throughout the decades, the top 40s represented the majority of women's trends—not the exceptions.

ARCHETYPES OF WOMEN'S DEVELOPMENT IN POPULAR MUSIC

Era	Archetype	Archetypal Theme	Icon
1900–1929	Dependent/ Martyr	Love	Mary Pickford's film roles Greta Garbo
1930–1939	Innocent/Victim	Love	Betty Boop Billie Holliday
1940–1949	Wonder Woman	Aspiration	Rosie the Riveter Katharine Hepburn
	Yearning/ Jezebel	Love	Judy Garland Mildred Pierce Tokyo Rose
1950–1959	Compliant/ Jezebel	Love	Harriet Nelson Marilyn Monroe Doris Day
1960–1969	Social/Rebel	War	Janis Joplin Gloria Steinem Betty Friedan
1970s through early 1980s	Wonder Woman/ Cynic	War/ Aspiration	TV's Wonder Woman Bionic Woman Tina Turner Princess Diana
Late 1980s	Assertive/	Aspiration	Dr. Sally Ride Whoopi Goldberg
	Sexpot	Wisdom	Cyndi Lauper Madonna
1990s	Lilith/Responsible adult	Wisdom	Oprah Winfrey Gloria Estefan Carly Fiorina

OUR STORY, TOO

As I did the research, it dawned on me that this was the story of *my* generation, too—at least for the last half of the century. I grew up in the 1950s and 1960s—like other baby boomers—listening over and over to Debbie Reynolds singing how Tammy (1957, no. 1) is in love, and I crooned along with Patience and Prudence, believing, as they did, that "Tonight You Belong to Me" (1956, no. 4). I rushed home from school each day to watch my idol, Annette, on *The Mickey Mouse Club* and bought her first hit single, "Tall Paul," which hit number seven in 1959. I was too young and innocent to understand the real meaning of the Shirelles' number-one 1962 hit, "Will You Love Me Tomorrow," but I had enough crushes on various boys to sing along with their 1961 "Dedicated to the One I Love," who was sometimes my "Johnny Angel" (a 1962 hit by Shelley Fabares, who also starred in *The Donna Reed Show*). In college in 1968, I could really relate to the themes in Vikki Carr's song "It Must Be Him." I was needy and completely unconscious about my own strength.

So, this is a book about how popular music speaks to the deeper feelings and longings within ourselves—to our archetypes. It is not a book particularly about female singers or songwriters, as others have done that subject well. Instead, I wanted to look at the songs identified with women singers that were very popular, those that hit the Top 40 charts. In the early years of the century, songs were charted by sales of sheet music, lists from the American Society of Composers, Authors, and Publishers (ASCAP), music periodicals, and several music hit books. As the years progressed, record sales and radio play took precedence, and by 1939 *Billboard* had established itself as the definitive source for charted songs. Pre-1939 chart information was not as consistently available, except for the forty songs that were the most popular of each year. Following *Billboard*'s ascendance in 1939, all Top 40 songs were charted, which actually resulted in anywhere from ninety-nine to over three hundred charted songs per year. In other words, every song that hit number one, every number two, and so on was featured in *Billboard*'s lists.

Of all the thousands of songs recorded each year, why were certain ones more popular? The ones that hit the Top 40, and certainly the Top Ten, say more about our culture than they do about a particular singer or songwriter. For example, in 1966, Nancy Sinatra's "These Boots Are Made for Walkin'" hit number one, while the Ronettes' "I Can Hear Music" only got to one hundred. Or why did 1972 have number-one hits of "I Am Woman" and "You're So Vain" by Carly Simon, while number ninety was "Open the Door" by Judy Collins?

Songs that were embraced by society-at-large are a kind of Rorschach test for the culture of that time. We can use popular music as a mirror to hold up to ourselves, to see who we are.

So it is not who wrote those songs that's relevant, whether male or female. We are looking instead at which songs were an indicator of our values, perceptions, and longings. Because the songs that sold the most tell us how we see the world. Yet that influence moved in both directions. That is, the values of the culture determined, to some extent, which songs became popular. But by listening to those tunes over and over, we were influenced by those messages; our values were shaped.

To be sure, songs sell for a number of reasons besides lyrics, including singer, melody, and beat. Some people aren't even completely aware of the lyrics of songs.

Studies show that men and women relate differently to music. While men are more aware of the melody and beat, women, on the other hand, listen to the lyrics first and the melody second. According to a study done by Larry Rosin of Edison Media Research in Somerville, New Jersey, women are much more lyrically driven and pay more attention to the story of the song. He also found that women hear higher and lower frequencies than men, who prefer upbeat rhythm songs. Because they are more focused on the melody and beat, men prefer much louder music than the more lyrics-oriented women (Dickerson 1998; Fisher 1999). That may explain why there are identifiable trends in female song themes throughout the century. It isn't accidental that there were virtually no songs about women's own strength until the sixties and now there are many such lyrics. And if you believe the work on subliminal advertising, then lyrics listened to over and over can make some long-lasting impact on our psyches, whether we are conscious of it or not.

We will trace the years from the early decades, when women had only a few percentage points of the top hits, up through the nineties, where at last women's pop music was getting on par with male singers. By 1996, women's music was finally outselling that sung by men (Dickerson 1998).

We have come a long way, baby.

ACKNOWLEDGMENTS

*T*he song from *Carousel* "You'll Never Walk Alone" could be rewritten for this project with the title "You'll Never Write Alone." Of the numerous books I have written, none has needed that collective process more than *RESPECT.* Incredible amounts of research were required, both in women's history and music, and I was blessed to have important collaborators.

Karen Streets-Anderson worked on this project for many months. A self-described popular-music junkie, she was perfectly suited to research lyrics and the impact songs had on society. Some of this came from her searches and some from her own experiences. At the end of the project, she told me with great intensity how much she loved this research. Content analysis of the lyrics was done not only by Susanne Fest, a researcher of extraordinary ability, with whom I have worked on several projects, but also by Kristi Skeeters, a young woman of great potential. Getting deep information on the history of women and work was done by Annette Alexander, who provided important insights. As we got launched, Debbie Waddell helped me with some of the early research, as did Joe Aniello and Maxcia Lizarraga. At Vanderbilt University, Director of Women's Studies

Ronnie Steinberg became a supporter, while Women's Center Director Linda Manning and Assistant Director Hilary Forbes arranged for me to present during women's history month. Mary Watson was a wonderful colleague, even after she moved to the New School in New York City. Kelly Christie at the Owen School loved this project and was a big supporter.

I must, though, give the deepest of appreciation to Ben Levy and the Rabbani Trust, who first asked me to do a presentation on the equality of men and women at a social and economic development conference. Because I had been experimenting with music in my leadership workshops, I decided to use a "few" songs for this presentation. Little did I know the music part would take on a life of its own. Before I knew it, I was mesmerized by the progression of messages in women's popular music throughout the century. A few months later, my writer's agent, John Willig, immediately saw the potential of this topic as a book. And so the project was born.

It took the vision of Myles Thompson at TEXERE to realize the potential of this book, which was further helped through the support of other TEXERE staff: Lee Thompson, Victoria Larson, Cricket O'Brien, Gail Blackhall, Virginia Rutter, and Renea Perry, who was so prompt in returning my many phone calls. Without the invaluable advice of developmental editor Mina Samuels, the book would look much different. And David Hahn and his staff provided expert PR help.

Various friends have given me needed emotional support and ideas throughout the project. Dale Finn and Kent Zimmerman were instrumental in getting me on stage the first time to do a woman's song. Marsha Day saw the potential early on and encouraged me, as did Susan Lewis Wright and Leslie Asplund, both highly competent artists. Mary Lynn Pulley advised me to follow my heart and pursue this work, leaving other, less satisfying endeavors. My music teachers, Gary and Robin Earl, helped my musical skills, as well as ideas for various songs. Bob and Debby Rosenfeld were encouraging, and Bob saw the usefulness of this material within organizations as training programs in diversity awareness. Lana Bogan was always there with love, Jennie Carter Thomas gave me more support than she could ever know, Cheri Shakiban Olver gave much love, and Mark and Maxine Rossman stayed, as ever, my longtime friends and buddies. Giving me hope and some valuable insights were my new friends: Holly Tashian, Nan Allison, Gail Reese, and Elizabeth Crook. Huge thanks are due to Barbara Hunt of USAA Corporation, who arranged for me to do my first large performance (four hundred people) of *A Musical History of Women and Work*, which helped me greatly in continuing the research for the book.

Professionally, I've gotten help from Gina Mendello, my project associate, Tracy Moor (who also did invaluable work securing permissions for lyrics), my marketing director, Kelly Clark, graphic artists Carolyn Stalcup and David Probst, as well as Kevin Madill, the pianist who scored my one-woman show, and Michael London, with whom I performed some gender and music presentations entitled "From Under His Thumb to I Am Woman." The laborious process of securing permissions for lyrics was helped by Tracy Moor, who saved the day for me as I got worn out. Both of us are eternally grateful to the many music licensing people we spoke to, especially Rosemarie Gawelko of Warner Music, who answered many questions.

And my family: My daughters (Roxanne, twenty; Solange, eighteen; and Elizabeth, sixteen) often gave me important feedback on the project. Roxanne stayed up all night toward the end of the project and helped me collect lyrics for the last decade. The deadline was looming and she was there for me when I really needed it. Solange and Elizabeth helped me to interpret rap lyrics, which made no sense to me. Elizabeth said they weren't supposed to make sense.

My sister, Janet, who always is there when I need her. Then my husband, Dick, who came to see how important this work was to me and what the potential impact could be, becoming my biggest coach and supporter. For his love I am most grateful (but *not* codependent!).

DOROTHY MARCIC
Nashville, Tennessee

FIRST MOVEMENT:
Invisible, Dependent, and Sexy

VERSE ONE
1900–1929

"I'll Cook and Pay the Rent so Long as He Stays with Me"

ARCHETYPES PRESENT:

Dependent/Martyr

*T*he predominant music themes that resonated throughout the early part of the last century were dependency and compliancy. There were also strains of resentment that presented themselves in a few songs as conniving women and threats to two-timing men.

Women were more or less invisible to public life around 1900. It hadn't changed much since 1848 when Elizabeth Cady Stanton wrote that married women were dead in the eyes of the law and were completely under the domination of their husbands. No woman could vote (New Zealand in 1893, Australia in 1902 preceded the 1919 U.S. granting of women the right to vote) and she was denied admittance to many universities and professions. Though vaudeville was thriving, it featured mostly male performers. For women to sing or dance on stage was seen in the same light as prostitution.

Marginalization of other groups occurred, as well. African-Americans were parodied in blackface with the popular minstrel shows, though all-black minstrel shows were popular, too. Millions of children toiled for ten hours a day and were seen as cheerful elves by factory owners. It is no surprise, then, that popular music was dominated by males, and generally white ones at that. Women had been closely connected with music since ancient times, but when it came to music in the public arena, they were mostly excluded. In some countries, that exclusion included the *forced* wearing of veils to cover themselves in public, a practice banned in 1923 in Turkey, though still practiced in some countries today. In other societies, young girls were forced to marry at young ages, at age eight or even younger. India worked toward more social justice when it passed 1929's Child Marriage Restraint Act, which forbid this practice; unfortunately, however, it still has not been completely eliminated. China, not long after in 1934, banned the practice of binding women's feet. It's surprising how many ancient coercive practices had held on the way into the twentieth century.

There had been some women in popular music previously, most notably the Swedish soprano Jenny Lind, who toured the United States in 1850–52 under the auspices of Phineas T. Barnum. But mostly it was about men. Popular music in the early years of the century included male barbershop quartets, ragtime songs, minstrel tunes, brass marching bands (such as John Philip Sousa's), parlor songs, as "In the Shade of the Old Apple Tree" (1905) and "I Wonder Who's Kissing Her Now" (1909). The most popular composer back then was George M. Cohan, best known for such tunes as the 1905 hit "Yankee Doodle Boy." With all those white males singing up a storm, it took a beautiful and courageous foreign woman, who later became a U.S. citizen, to capture the heart of America. British singer and actress Lillie Langtry, also known for her affair with the future King Edward VII, toured the United States in 1888 and 1904, and many times afterward, gaining her first "groupie" in Texas's notorious Judge Roy Bean. Though Lillie did not accept the rigid rules for feminine conduct (she casually entered establishments listed "for men only"), she nonetheless was confined to the common fashion of her day, the corset, a symbol of female restriction that would take more time to be collectively thrown off—during World War I, largely through the work of Coco Chanel, whose clothing freed women with more liberating styles of simple suits, sweaters, and the "little black dress." In 1900, though, the ideal of womanhood was to marry no later than age twenty-one with a waist size equaling her number of years in age. Nothing was more attractive than an infinitesimal waist and large hips, made more so with generous padding.

It was also a time of change. Immigrants were coming to the States by the millions (about 10 million per year), swelling the population by 50 percent from 1880 to 1900, to 76 million. My grandmother, Dorothy Nelson (later Stordock), was one of those immigrants, who left Norway, alone, in 1909 at age sixteen to come to the land of plenty, the land where people told her "gold hung off the trees." She was typical of the millions processed at Ellis Island in those days. Dorothy was young, from a poor family (her fisherman father had died before she was born, and her grandmother raised Dorothy). Though she spoke no English, Dorothy was determined to make a good life for herself in the promised land. Her first job was as a maid in Illinois; within a few years she married my grandfather and they took up farming, staying on the farm for decades despite changing trends.

By 1900 more people were moving to the cities, attracted by industrial jobs. In 1880, almost 60 percent of the U.S. employed population were farmworkers. That dropped to 37.5 percent by 1900 (and further to 1.6 percent by 1990). This influenced the role of women in families and society. On the farm, women had a clear role as farm wife, with prescribed duties. But what did this mean to a newly moved city family?

We can see a glimmer of the changes to come, too. The year 1900 was the first time women were allowed to participate in the Olympics, even if it was a mere nineteen females in two events, golf and tennis. These Paris games had a total of 1,225 athletes, making women 1.5 percent of the total. Education was opening up, too. By the turn of the century, one-third of college students were women. Yet what they were taught was designed to perpetuate the status quo. The earliest women's colleges, in fact, were started to help prepare women for marriage, motherhood, and service to Christianity. An unintended consequence of this education showed itself soon. Once those women went to college, they started gaining self-confidence and assertion. They began to chafe under the Victorian requirements that women never sweat or exert themselves, and they took up bicycling with a vengeance (but did so with great difficulty in the still-common corsets).

Though the emphasis may have been on marriage as a full-time occupation, women were increasingly part of the paid labor force. By 1900, 38 percent of families depended at least partly on women's paid labor. Of women ages sixteen to twenty, one-half worked for wages. Thirty-five percent of professional workers were female.

As the twentieth century dawned, a revolution was taking place in society and business. Every sector was more complex and the "search for order" became the motivating force of the era for factories, small businesses, municipalities, and politicians. The overriding solution to many problems became so-called scientific management, one of whose early developers was Dr. Lillian Gilbreth, who with her husband, Frank, did the early time-and-motion studies. She has been referred to as the first superwoman—combining career and family, the mother of twelve—whose story was immortalized in the movie *Cheaper by the Dozen*. Receiving her doctorate at Brown University in 1915, she had four children in tow at the ceremony. Another great thinker of business solutions was Mary Parker Follett, who has recently been rediscovered by management professionals.

More technology resulted in a radical transformation of office work. The complexities of business required more clerical staff, bookkeepers, and accountants. And women took on the challenge. In

1900, one of the few occupations open to women was teaching, and 70 percent of employed women were teachers. That soon changed. While women made up just 6 percent of the bookkeepers in 1880, they had swelled to 31 percent by 1910 and 63 percent by 1930. Accounting positions were seen as unsuitable for women, because they had to travel a great deal, spending time in boardinghouses and hotels. By World War I, though, accountants were able to work most of the year from the home office, and at least a few women went into the profession. With all the women in office work today, it seems incredible that women were initially suspected of not being able to do this kind of work at all. Many companies resisted this trend in the early years of the century. Aetna Insurance Company became one of the first in its industry to hire female clerks, who nonetheless had to use the back elevator in order not to offend male executives.

Even so, office work became gender-polarized, and women were increasingly in clerical and stenographer positions. But women had greater talents than being left to the bottom of the organizational ladder. Because women were entering college at rapid rates since the time they had been allowed to matriculate, there was a fear of the "feminization" of higher education. No wonder. Women achieved greatly when given the chance. At the turn of the century, women were receiving up to 56 percent of all Phi Beta Kappa and other awards at some universities. Even with that, the prevailing thoughts of the day were that men had a more varied intelligence than women, which justified men's monopoly on the most important occupations and positions.

So quotas at universities began, designed to keep women out of the most prestigious programs. Because office work was becoming more complex, the newly developed positions of "manager" were often limited to graduates of business programs, which, with few exceptions, only admitted men. Women were allowed to enter into programs for clerical work, which they took on and did quite well.

Women on the factory line wanted more, too. As a sign of the dormant strength rearing its head, twenty thousand female garment workers went on strike in 1909 to protest intolerable working conditions. It didn't help much. Two years later, in 1911, dangerous working conditions caused a fire in the Triangle Shirtwaist Company and the death of over 140 young immigrant women.

Margaret Sanger chafed, too, but for other reasons. One of eleven children, Sanger blamed her mother's premature demise on her body being weakened by frequent pregnancies. Trained as a nurse, she began to see that smaller family size was better for a number of reasons. In 1912 *The Woman Rebel* began publication, including articles about birth control, and writer-publisher Sanger was quickly arrested under obscenity charges. Her first birth-control clinic was shut down nine days after it opened in 1916. Finally, in 1923, she was able to open a legal clinic. That was the same year the Equal Rights Amendment was first introduced in Congress (it was not passed until 1972, but was never ratified).

Other women were emerging as leaders, showing that women had untapped potential. Even if there were only a handful, at least it was a start. Polish scientist Marie Curie won the Nobel Prize, twice, in 1903 and 1911. Nellie Bly pioneered what we now call investigative journalism as a reporter at Joseph Pulitzer's *New York World*, once going undercover for ten days as a patient in a mental institution. Later in her life, she took over as CEO of her husband's multimillion-dollar iron-clad factory after he died, and was one of the first to recognize the importance of treating workers decently. In 1899, Jane Addams founded Chicago's world-famous settlement house—Hull House—which became a center for social programs in the early years of the new century. As a tireless reformer, Addams was responsible for helping laws get passed on child labor and women's rights, and she received the Nobel Peace Prize in 1931 for her efforts to end war. The only American woman to found a lasting religion, Mary Baker Eddy overcame personal tragedies to develop Christian Science and then started in 1908 the still-published *Christian Science Monitor.*

Nebraskan Willa Cather wrote numerous successful novels about strong women, the most famous being *O Pioneers!* in 1913. Educational reformer Maria Montessori opened her first school in the slums of Rome in 1907. "America's Sweetheart" Mary Pickford may have played the Compliant on the screen, knowing that archetype sold movie tickets, but behind the scenes she became a powerful studio mogul, starting in 1919.

There were other evidences of tiny saplings of strength. Women worked hard to end the scourge that alcoholism brought to families. (They had a point. The cost to society of alcoholism—from health care, lost productivity, and premature death—was $246 billion in 1992.) Back in the early part of the century, women thought temperance, or the prohibition of alcohol, would improve the situation. Another area of activism occurred with southern women, who toiled for fifty years, starting in 1890, to end lynching.

During these early decades, a few women became visible in popular music. Fanny Brice was signed to the Ziegfeld Follies in 1910. She was a more earthy performer, more connected to the average person than the previous female musical success model of the operatic and dignified Jenny Lind, or the exotic foreigner Lillie Langtry.

But women were still in a one-down position. In fact, she was way down, and the few popular songs about women's place of that time showed that all too clearly. One was the 1902 number-two song "Bill Bailey, Won't You Please Come Home," written by Hughie Cannon. Though it was sung by a man, Arthur Collins, it was the first hit of the century that spoke about women's power and was sung from the point of view of the woman. It was later associated with Ella Fitzgerald. It's interesting that in those first two decades, the only Top 40 song that dealt with women's power was sung by a male. It was too risky for women to speak out themselves.

"BILL BAILEY, WON'T YOU PLEASE COME HOME"
Won't you come home Bill Bailey, won't you come home?
She moans the whole day long.
I'll do the cookin', darlin', I'll pay the rent.
I know I done you wrong
Do you remember that rainy evenin'
I threw you out, with nothin' but a fine tooth comb?
Ya, I know I'm to blame, ain't it a shame.
Bill Bailey won't you please come home?

She had exerted some power by throwing the scoundrel out, but then, in her apparent neediness as the victim, she begs him to come back, promising to take care of all his needs. Her needs go unnoticed and unmet. It was the story of my grandmother's marriage to Oscar Stordock, an alcoholic, unable to support the family. After years of putting up with his drunkenness, Dorothy Stordock finally threw him out and she was left to support five children completely alone. She had to leave the farm and move into the city to find work. Twenty years later she got a postcard from him, asking her to take him back. My grandmother drove from Beloit, Wisconsin, to Chicago and found Oscar on skid row and brought him back home. Because that's what women did.

Though women had few charted hits in those years, some of their songs became classics, loved and played for many years. Many of the songs women sang back then had no themes of their own power. They were often love songs that made the singer an observer to life, as in "Shine on Harvest Moon," in which the lyrics talk about wanting the moon to shine strong, so the singer might be given some love. It is the voice of a Compliant, wanting forces outside herself to make her life better.

ℛEMINISCENCE

"Shine on Harvest Moon,"
Elise Stephenson, 1909, no. 1

My sister and three brothers and I would stand around doing dishes after dinner. Because we were poor and didn't have much in the way of entertainment, we sang to each other. Hitting notes and harmonies as we passed dishes from pan to the person with the dish towel. We'd sing "Shine on Harvest Moon," "Irene" (1920, no. 3), and many others.

When I grew up, I moved to Milwaukee to work. My brother Donald enlisted in the army during World War II. He got stationed during the early years at Camp Douglas, which is near Chicago. Once or twice a month Donald had leave and came to visit me. It would be just the two of us then, singing away after dinner and doing dishes. Oh, I loved it when our voices blended, standing there in front of the sink. As we sang, I wanted the moon to shine down on us, make our lives better, and make my brother safe in the war.

Leone Evert, as told to her daughter
PEWAUKEE, WISCONSIN

The century's first decade had scant hit songs by women. With forty-nine single or duet Top 40 songs, Ada Jones was the only female artist to hit it really big, singing "I Just Can't Make My Eyes Behave" (1907, no. 1) in the presence of "My Irish Rosie" (1907, no. 2), to whom I ask, "Wouldn't You Like to Have Me for a Sweetheart?" (1908, no. 6). Or at least, as Jones sings, "Please Come and Play in My Yard" (1905, no. 6) because I finally want to say that "I've Got Rings on My Fingers" (1909, no. 1). Differences in racial consciousness is evident in her song "If the Man in the Moon Were a Coon" (1907, no. 3). She was best known as a vaudevillian impressionist especially skilled in various dialects (Italian, German, Irish, African-American) and personas (a Bowery tough girl, an Irish colleen, a cowgirl). In other words, she became famous by becoming other people, rather than by being herself.

Though a few more women were recording top hits in the second decade, they still accounted for only about 10 percent of the songs on the charts. Many of them were sentimental love songs. Just to give you an idea of what the themes of those kinds of songs were back then, here are some examples: Elida Morris crooned to "Stop, Stop, Stop (Come on Over and Love Me Some More)" (1911, no. 4) and then "Kiss Me, My Honey Kiss Me" (1910, no. 4) on "Moonlight Bay" (Dolly Connolly, 1912, no. 3) where we can "Say Not Love Is a Dream" (Olive Kline, 1913, no. 4), but I don't want to pay "The High Cost of Loving" (Elida Morris, 1914, no. 8).

Or else they might have been folksy and nostalgic tunes such as Elida Morris's 1914 number-three hit "I Want to Go Back to Michigan (Down on the Farm)" or maybe to "My Old Kentucky Home" (Alma Gluck, 1916, no. 3) where I'll see "The Old Folks at Home/Swanee River" (Alma Gluck, 1915, no. 3). If that doesn't work, Alma Gluck asks to "Carry Me Back to Old Virginny" (1915, no. 1), where I can "Listen to the Mockingbird" (1916, no. 3). These songs demonstrate the yearning for a life other than the one she had.

A few songs did address the power imbalance in relationships. In the teens, Sophie Tucker had five Top 40 hits with a lot a lovin', for she wanted "That Lovin' Rag" (1910, no. 3) and "That Lovin' Two-Step Man" (1910, no. 9) to give her "That Loving Soul Kiss" (1911, no. 8) in "Some of These Days" (her most famous song, 1911, no. 2).

The Great World War and its aftermath brought hit patriotic tunes for women, with Nora Bayes looking to "Over There" (1917, no. 1) and asking in 1919, "How You Gonna Keep 'em Down on the Farm (After They've Seen Paree)?" (no. 2). The Farber Sisters wondered "If He Can Fight Like He Can Love (Good Night, Germany)" (1918, no. 3).

The vote was won. Then the earth shifted. In 1920, after the Suffragists' difficult seventy-year struggle, the Nineteenth Amendment to the U.S. Constitution was ratified, giving women the right to vote. Also in 1920, Czechoslovakia and Albania passed female suffrage. Other countries that had recently given women the right to vote included Finland in 1906; Norway in 1913; Denmark in 1915; Austria, Canada, Poland, Russia and over-thirty women in the UK in 1918; and Germany, Holland, and Sweden in 1919.

Suddenly women's voices were allowed in public forums. But the effects were not as tumultuous as expected. The suffragists scattered to the winds on varying and often competing causes. And women did not take to the polls immediately. In fact, it was not until 1957 that women accounted for 50 percent of the voters.

But the tremor of this new change was felt somewhere. Defenses appeared against what must have seemed like the female threat. Medical schools started restricting the number of women students to 5 percent, which reduced the number of female physicians throughout the 1920s. So, the Nineteenth Amendment created further insecurity in the nation, a fear that those brassy, man-hating feminists (sound familiar?) would take over. After all, women were smoking and drinking in public and exhibited a more open sexuality, which fit in with the wild, speakeasy image of society.

It was a heady time for women. Because there were now increasing numbers of female college graduates, and because women had done so well in men's work during World War I, there was this feeling that women could do anything, any kind of work. Numerous female writers of the day noted how women were thankful for the work of early pioneers, how there was no limit to their future possibilities, and how they assumed that everywhere managerial and professional jobs would be open to them. The reality hit hard and painfully. Even as late as 1919, women were barred from about 70 percent of civil service exams for scientific, mechanical, or managerial positions. Leaders of business and higher education came out publicly against women taking on positions with any authority. That, after all, was a male domain—and a white one, at that.

To add further to the difficulties, women's appearance was under constant scrutiny by supervisors. They had to look nice, which is one reason younger females often had preference in hiring. On the other hand, many employers believed short hair and dresses distracted male employees; therefore they developed strict dress codes for women.

With all the successes and struggles for females, songs about women and power continued with the theme of dependency. The society needed to reassure itself that women were not going to revolt en masse. Musical theater aided this reassurance. Broadway shows had gone through a recent transition from visual and auditory spectacles to plays with themes, and now the songs had more meaning than previous Broadway tunes. Take a look at the 1926 George and Ira Gershwin song (still popular today) from the Broadway hit *Oh, Kay!*

"SOMEONE TO WATCH OVER ME"
There's a somebody I'm longing to see
I hope that he turns out to be
Someone who'll watch over me
I'm a little lamb who's lost in a wood
I know I could always be good
To one who'll watch over me

Which "little lamb lost in the wood" is going to upset the status quo? The flappers may have had an image of independence, but they were considered floozies. Good women were dependent. So, the message from this enduring tune is: Take care of me because I am helpless. I am Compliant. And if you hurt me, well, that's what men do, as we see in the next song. Fanny Brice's 1922 number-ten song "My Man" shows how she accepts the role of betrayed and battered wife and comes back for more. This song is believed to be autobiographical—about her second husband, gambler and gangster Nicky Arnstein.

"MY MAN"
Two or three girls has he
That he likes as well as me
But I love him
I don't know why I should
He isn't good
He isn't true
He beats me too
What can I do?. . .
What's the difference if I say
I'll go away
When I know I'll come back
On my knees some day

When she says, "He beats me too/What can I do?" it is not merely poetic license. Back in the 1920s men could beat their wives without fear of legal consequences. She really *was* helpless to defend herself or be her own person. No wonder she was so dependent. There was no other choice.

People are shocked when they hear these lyrics. Many of them have heard Barbra Streisand's modernized version of "My Man" (1965, no. 79), which left out the crucial lines of "He beats me too/What can I do?" When people hear those words, they gasp. How is it possible that such lyrics were in this classic and popular song? Because it appealed to what was (and still is, in some quarters) the reality of a woman in love.

Movies reflected these concepts, too. Lillian Gish played parts as a waiflike woman, ready for a man to rescue her, while "America's Sweetheart" Mary Pickford often portrayed a smart though clumsy woman who saw social mobility through the love of a rich man.

Torch singer extraordinaire and Ziegfeld Follies star Ruth Etting did a good job of selling songs with Compliant themes. Of her sixty-two charted songs, a significant number were of the he-done-me-wrong-and-what-a-victim-I-am variety. She was excited about her man and sang "Let's Talk about My Sweetie" (1926, no. 14), but after a while the glow was gone and she moaned to him: You're "Mean to Me" (1929, no. 3) and describes the perverse pleasure her man takes in humiliating her in public or private. She told how "Lonesome and Sorry" (1926, no. 3) she was because "I'm Nobody's Baby" (1927, no. 9) and "My Blackbirds Are Bluebirds Now" (1928, no. 9). Maybe she got into the funk that often because her motto was "It All Depends on You" (1927, no. 8), because "I'll Get By" (1929, no. 3) no matter what, as long as I have you, which led to "What I Wouldn't Do for That Man" (1929, no. 9) and "I'm Good for Nothing but Love" (1931, no. 7). When Etting sang with such authentic emotion on these subjects, she was singing from experience; her tumultuous life was chronicled in the Doris Day–James Cagney movie whose title is the name of Etting's signature song, "Love Me or Leave Me."

The idea of a man being cruel on the outside but really and truly loving her on the inside is an enduring one, and it is the basis of most romance novels. It is closely linked to all those horror movies about men who change from Good Guy (Dr. Jekyll) to Creep (Mr. Hyde). The fact that these horror movies were popular from as early as 1908 and included other titles such as *Werewolf* (1913), *Dracula* (1931), and *Phantom of the Opera* (1925) shows just how far we will go to excuse beastly behavior in men.

Music and horror films often rationalized abusive behavior back in that era. The Weimar Republic in Germany was spinning out of control and creating a vacuum into which a ruthless Adolf Hitler would later ascend. It is no coincidence that the late teens and 1920s were a time of creepy expressionistic German horror films, such as *The Cabinet of Dr. Caligari* (1919), *The Eyes of the Mummy* (1918), *Dr. Mabuse, The Gambler* (1922), and *Nosferatu* (1922).

If women weren't the dependent doormat ready to be walked all over, then they were shown to be manipulative and cruel—a true Jezebel—

and you'd better watch out. Dolly Kay's number-three hit in 1924 (coincidentally the same year Nellie Taylor Ross of Wyoming became the first woman elected as state governor) told us the *real* truth about a certain type of woman. The song is trying to tell us that any woman who is strong and stands up to a man is really a witch (or that other, rhyming word that starts with "b") and is mean clear-through. It was an era of two choices for females, the old Madonna-whore dichotomy. Either be the dependent doormat Compliant, or else be branded a Hard Hearted Hannah—the mean Jezebel.

"HARD HEARTED HANNAH"
They call her Hard Hearted Hannah, the vamp of Savannah,
The meanest gal in town
Leather is tough, but Hannah's heart is tougher
She's a gal who loves to see men suffer
To tease 'em and thrill 'em, to torture and kill 'em
Is her delight they say.
I saw her at the seashore with a great big pan
There was Hannah pouring water on a drowning man
She's Hard Hearted Hannah, the vamp of Savannah G. A.

The voice is clear from the singer, who in no way identifies with Hannah, that any woman who might stand up to a man, or reject his affections, will easily be labeled as hard and cruel—a Jezebel.

But there was another voice appearing, the blues, which took off in the 1920s. The radio had brisk sales from 1921, which caused a brief downturn in record sales. It meant, though, that more people were listening to music more of the time; therefore, greater diffusion of trends was possible. This was the so-called Jazz Age, associated with new kinds of musical beats and harmonies and even different rules of music. Part of these changes was the introduction of a genre known as the blues. Historians trace blues' origins to Africa and then to the rural South, African-American sharecropper experience.

Because of the harsh economic and racial oppression in the Mississippi Delta region, the Delta blues is considered to be the most intense version.

After the civil war, former slaves drifted northward by the hundreds of thousands. Many went to Chicago and helped diffuse this new musical form, which took shape there as Chicago blues. Ma Rainey and other black vaudevillians started recording blues records, some of which hit the Top 40. Blues singer Mamie Smith had eight Top 40 songs, including her 1920 "Crazy Blues," which is considered the first authentic blues record and hit the charts at number three in 1921. In fact, though solo guitar-backed men had great influence in the blues, it was women whose voluminous recordings became known as classic blues, which was distinct with its characteristic small jazz group backup. The influence of these women was far-reaching. Though now widely regarded as one of the most important blues singers of that era, Ma Rainey had only one Top 40 hit. Her number-fourteen "See See Rider Blues" (1925, with Louis Armstrong on trumpet) was later recorded by a number of other artists, sometimes with the title "C.C. Rider" or "Jenny Take a Ride," including Chuck Willis (1957, no. 12), Lavern Baker (1963, no. 34), Eric Burdon and the Animals (1966, no. 10), Mitch Ryder and the Detroit Wheels (1965, no. 10) as well as Elvis Presley's uncharted version. CC-Rider is even the name of a software program allowing the generation of source code documentation. Ma Rainey also recorded other moderately popular songs, which were precursors to the later angry songs of the 1960s, such as "Trust No Man" (1924).

The popular culture started buying enough blues records in the twenties to make them hits, and several women became blues queens, who offered another view of life. It was another voice poking through the silver lining of the clouds of denial. The Roaring Twenties may have had lots of fun and wild abandonment, but it also brought the grittier parts of life to the surface. And for women, this was the first time their suffering was documented in Top 40 tunes. They told a very different story than Irene Bordoni's 1924 number-four song "So This Is Love," or 1925's number-two "Yes Sir That's My Baby," or Ruth Etting's 1929 number-three hit, "I'll Get By as Long as I Have You."

The blues, born out of centuries of oppression of African-Americans, was about pain, loss, and being mistreated. Some have said that a happy, well-to-do person is incapable of writing or even singing the blues, because it requires deep, deep pain from within. "Empress of the Blues" Bessie Smith, protégé of Ma Rainey, was the most influential female blues singer of the 1920s, scoring sixteen Top 40 hits. Her 1923 number-one hit "Down-Hearted Blues" wasn't counting tea for two or looking on the sunny side of the street. Rather, it had that you-done-me-wrong theme that had a stronger basis in reality than many of the overly optimistic tunes women were singing in this decade, and she defined the style with her own unique phrasing.

"DOWN-HEARTED BLUES"
Gee, but it's hard to love someone
When that someone don't love you!
I'm so disgusted, heart-broken, too;
I've got those down-hearted blues;
Once I was crazy 'bout a man;
He mistreated me all the time,
The next man I get has got to promise me
To be mine, all mine!

This song could be part two of "Someone to Watch Over Me," for it tells us how she feels when he *doesn't* watch over her, when he does *not* love her as expected. That's when she feels betrayed and sings the down-hearted blues, later noting that "A Good Man Is Hard to Find" (1928, no. 13). A number of her hits were later rerecorded by other artists and became hits again. These included "I Ain't Got Nobody" (1926, no. 8; recorded by David Lee Roth in 1985, no. 12), "After You've Gone" (1927, no. 7, and recorded by numerous artists, such as

Louis Armstrong in 1932 at no. 15 and Benny Goodman in 1935 at no. 20, as well as other non-charted versions by Bette Midler and others), and "Nobody Knows You When You're Down and Out" (1929, no. 15, and recorded by Nina Simone in 1960 at no. 60). Even though a few of these had already been done, Smith's rendition of them gave the songs a new verve.

Angela Davis (remember her from the 1960s radical era? Now she's a professor at the University of California at Santa Cruz) wrote about how the blues were a means of African-American women maintaining their identity and sanity—and their strength. If you listen to the words carefully, you will see that many of the blues songs have a sentence or two indicating their own strength, plus they show an inner power when they sing. One reason blues songs, and even codependent ones, can become a source of healing is that they allow the mistreated one to name the pain, an important step in therapy.

A white version of the blues was sung by Marion Harris (though some would argue that most white women had no business even *trying* to sing the blues). But she was not, in essence, a blues singer, because many of her songs were of that common smiley-face quality. She told people to "Look for the Silver Lining" (1921, no. 1) because "Some Sunny Day" (1922, no. 3) you'll have "Tea for Two" (1925, no. 1). These were quite different in tone than her darker tunes, such as "I Ain't Got Nobody" (1921, no. 3), but in case I do, I'll be "Aggravatin' Papa" (1923, no. 3, and also recorded by Bessie Smith, whose version reached no. 12 that year, and Sophie Tucker, who got to no. 10 with it).

"AGGRAVATIN' PAPA"
Aggravatin' Papa, don't try to two-time me!
Aggravatin' Papa, treat me kind or let me be;
Listen while I get you told,
Stop messin' round with my jellyroll,
If I catch you out with your high-brown baby,
I'll smack you down, and I don't mean maybe!

Aggravatin' Papa, I'll do anything you say,
But when you start to running, don't you run around my way;
Now, Papa, treat me pretty, nice and sweet,
'Cause I possess a forty-four that don't repeat,
So, Aggravatin' Papa, don't try to two-time me!"

This song has an element of the common Compliant theme: "I'll do anything you say." But it mixes it with threats ("I'll smack you down") and cajoling ("treat me pretty"), and therefore the message does not come out of an inner strength. It is more like a child who begs to be loved, but then throws a tantrum when things go wrong. So even though the blues, on the surface, seems to capture more strength in women, it is actually more of the dependent female who feels betrayed and then gets ornery when the man does not fill her needs. At the same time, the lack of denial in these songs, the willingess to name the pain, can be seen as a therapeutic process and do indicate more strength than doormat songs.

The other well-known southern music was gospel. But whereas gospel music required group collaboration, the blues was more of an individual activity and spoke to the harsher side of life. Blues singers weren't waiting for the Lord to lift them up to heaven. They were bemoaning the pains and sufferings of life. In the early days of blues, African-Americans divided themselves into the God-fearing folks who sang religious songs and those who preferred that "devil music." Women sang the blues in the rural South, too. Their work was also often solitary—cooking, cleaning, gardening, and child rearing—and the blues became their solace and even sometimes lullabies for the children.

Only three women turned up in the lists of top artists of the twenties. Number seven Marion Harris (Ruth Etting was no. 19 and Nora Bayes was no. 28) had amazing influence. Still, her positive persona touched the culture deeper. Of her thirteen Top 40 hits of the decade, five were bluesy and eight were more happy-face. One of the more enduring songs of Marion Harris was "It Had to Be You," which would go on to be rerecorded over and over, hitting the Top 40 another eleven times.

The theme of true love, with some compliance, was one that kept selling throughout the early 1900s. Most people don't remember the part of the song that asks: Why does she always give him his way? Why does she do just as he says? She wandered around and then finally found someone who would love her, even though he had lots of faults. Below is a story of a woman who lived that song. With multiple divorces, she thought she would never again find someone, faults or not, who could make her happy. Her more modern version of the song did not include becoming his codependent doormat, but rather an equal partner. In fact, she didn't wait for him to propose marriage. She told me that after she realized he was the one for her to marry, she kept singing "It Had to Be You" over and over again.

ℛEMINISCENCE

"It Had to Be You,"
Marion Harris, 1924, no. 3

I met Ed and his wife, Anita, in 1969 Omaha, as we would attend religious services together. Our kids played together. My daughters even had a nickname for him: Edward Bear. Little did I know back then how our lives would entwine twenty-five years hence.

Then I married my second husband and they moved to Panama and later to Nantucket. We kept in touch and saw each other occasionally. Everything changed after I divorced in 1991. Before I left for a posting in Siberia some months later, we had a nice long chat.

In March of 1993 I got a letter from a friend saying that Anita had recently died. It seemed impossible. She was quite vital when I saw her last. Then this gut feeling hit me, *I was going to marry Ed.* It embarrassed me and I tried to get it out of my mind. It wouldn't leave. I started to sing love songs when I was alone. "It Had to Be You." Where did that come from?

I left Siberia for a visit home that May. A friend told me, "Ed wants you to call." We talked about everything that had happened, Siberia, kids, Anita's death, how he was doing, and all the presentations about Siberia I was now giving. Ed and I had always had long talks. At the end of our conversation he said, "You know I'm not the kind to live alone. I see a snowfall, a beautiful sunset, it's nothing when I don't have anyone to share it with." I was about to tell him my gut feeling when he says, "I think I'd even marry an old grouch just so I didn't have to be alone." Did he think I was a grouch or was he not thinking of me at all?

Later that night, the gut feeling hit me even harder, "It Had to Be You." I went through everything, he was far from perfect, but it still felt like he was the one. Well I'd never been in love with him before, but he was the one I *knew* I was going to marry. I'd better tell him. But how could I think a several-times-divorced woman would really interest him? I started to pray to know God's will. I talked about it for hours with a good friend. No voice came to me out of the blue but I couldn't stand it. I figured I should at least tell him my intuition. It still took hours to get up the nerve.

I called one day after our last conversation, and he was surprised to hear from me this soon, but was very happy. I took a deep breath and said, "I have this gut feeling that someday we'll be married." There was a long pause. My heart was in my throat. Then he started with, "You can't mean it. You are too wonderful. You are such a good person. I yell a lot. I'm not a good person. I'm fat. I'm bald. You deserve

someone with money, I'm just a poor retired Air Force
sergeant." This sounded like a polite turndown till he turned
around immediately with, "But we have known each other
for twenty-five years. We have always been able to talk. We
have lots in common. You will love it here on Nantucket.
Anita was an artist too and she loved it. I will send you a
plane ticket and we can get married right away."

I immediately said, "Whoa! We need to move more
slowly." He disagreed about waiting and said, "Anita was
healthy and died of a cerebral hemorrhage in minutes. We
don't know how long we'll have; let's spend the time we have
together." He did agree that we should have more long talks
and gave me his telephone credit card.

We talked every night as I took care of my schedule of
public appearances and family gatherings, singing "It Had to
Be You" all the way. I had a space of eight days in my
schedule, and he flew me to Nantucket and we got married—
in July 1993. And since then we live happily ever after.

Andrea Dougan, artist
NANTUCKET, MASSACHUSETTS

Women had one-tenth of the Top 40 hits in this decade, and only
one-fifth of those had a bluesy quality, which means most of them
were either happy-go-lucky or sentimental love songs. So, even
though the blues offered another, more realistic view, it was nearly
drowned out by the "Button Up Your Overcoat" (Ruth Etting, 1929,
no. 15) songs all too prevalent back then.

Another influence of the 1920s was the singer Helen Kane, whose
1928 number-two hit "I Wanna Be Loved by You" helped shape the
future. She became the template for the 1930 birth of Betty Boop,
scantily clad with a baby-talk voice, destined to become the most
enduring female animated cartoon character of the century, and who
was to set a new standard for female perfection.

VERSE TWO
1930–1939

"Innocent Sexpot Betty Boop and the Songs of the Depression"

ARCHETYPES PRESENT:

Innocent/Victim

*C*odependence covered up with incessant cheerfulness dominated the music in this interwar period. Women were innocent and saw themselves as victims—they thought life was meaningless without a man and offered their love at any cost. Race issues also came to the fore in music.

The world would never be the same after two momentous events of the late 1920s. Warner Brothers released the first talking picture, *The Jazz Singer* with Al Jolson, in 1927. Two years later, in October of 1929, the stock market crashed and brought ten years of worldwide economic depression. The combination of talking pictures and bleak times created desire for escapism in entertainment, partly met by the new "talking cartoons." The desire to flee the grim realities around surely was one motivation for the 1930's invention of the singing telegram.

Animated cartoons had been around for some time, increasingly used in vaudeville theaters as "dumb acts." Max and David Fleischer were the first to experiment with sound and animation and created the future Betty Boop in the 1930 cartoon *Dizzy Dishes.* At first, Betty was a human-looking dog, with loads of spit curls. Depicted as a torch singer, she ended her songs with "boop-oop-a-doop," a definite imitation of singer and Paramount stock player Helen Kane. In fact, Kane sued the Fleischers but lost, since Betty was seen as the generic portrait of the late 1920's flapper.

By 1932 the nation's income had been cut in half, and Betty Boop was given her name and had become a human, dropping her dog ears. Until the Hayes Code was enforced in 1934, Betty was scantily dressed, provocative, and flirtatious. The Depression hung in the air, and Prohibition was not repealed until 1933. The fringes of lawlessness and breaking the rules were still common. With the same baby voice of Helen Kane, Betty Boop made 131 films, more than Mickey Mouse, and is considered to be the only animated superstar of the century. All her movies were musicals. Why was she popular? Some say because she was three parts Mae West and one part Shirley Temple. Even her signature song shows the complexity of her character.

"I Wanna Be Loved by You"
I wanna be loved by you, just you
And nobody else but you
I wanna be loved by you alone.

I wanna be kissed by you just you
And nobody else but you
I wanna be kissed by you alone.

I wouldn't aspire to anything higher
Than fill a desire to make you my own.

. . . boop oop a doop.

She wants to love and kiss, and she also wishes for codependency—having her highest goal be to fill another's needs. When she sings, it is with the baby voice of a Shirley Temple girl, but her clothes and manner are more Mae West. She wasn't touted for her intellect, either, for one of her favorite lines was, "I try to think, but nothing happens."

Of all the animated characters of this century, why is Betty Boop considered the only superstar? What was it about her that captured the imagination of the country enough for her to become this popular? I believe she touched some deep values about how the culture saw women, or rather, how it wanted women to be: sexy, provocative yet childlike, and dependent. Greta Garbo's silent films of the 1920s reflected the sexual allure of her character, but they showed a stronger woman, one who might challenge a male's ego. Boop, on the other hand, would be no threat to the existing power structure. And her popularity lasted for decades. I remember as a child in the 1950s watching so many Betty Boop cartoons on television that I had memorized a number of her songs and could still recite lines forty years later. To this day she has adoring followers, with numerous fan clubs and Web sites. Her archetype of sexy-child Compliant has endured throughout the century, too, including other stars such as Marilyn Monroe and Britney Spears.

Her success during the Depression probably helped her popularity as well, for people were longing for some escape from the struggles of daily life. Movies popular in that era were *King Kong* (1933), *Top Hat* (1935), with Fred Astaire and Ginger Rogers, Disney's *Snow White and the Seven Dwarfs* (1937), and *Gone with the Wind* (1939). At the same time, the languishing economy meant less disposable income to buy records. Add to that the proliferation of radios, with free music, and you end up with a deep depression in the record business in 1932. When Prohibition ended in 1933, it opened up new markets for clubs and bars, with many jukeboxes—which increased sales of records, saving the industry. The April 1935 debut of radio's

"Your Hit Parade" served to showcase the hottest tunes to the country, again helping record sales. In this same year, the so-called swing movement began eclipsing the blues and reducing women's participation in music, which explains the low percentage of women's songs on the charts.

Another reason women did poorly in the charts resulted from the decade's marked hostility toward women and women's issues, exacerbated by women taking on more of a public role. The more women did well, the greater the resistance. Eleanor Roosevelt, First Lady and social reformer, was often criticized for being so outspoken, for having her own opinion. It wasn't accepted for women to develop strength in athletics, either, particularly in the more nonfeminine sports. Babe Didrikson Zaharias won three gold medals in track and field at the 1932 Olympics and later won three U.S. Open golf championships. Because of her relentless pursuit of excellence and her tomboyish looks, she was reviled by many as a freak. Joe Williams of the *New York World-Telegram* wrote, "It would be much better if she and her ilk stayed at home, got themselves prettied up and waited for the phone to ring." In other words, she better see the light and become dependent on a man.

Despite so many obstacles, women continued to enter the workforce. In 1900, 70 percent of women workers were teachers, by 1930 that number was down to 58 percent. By that time women had entered business to such an extent that 45 percent of office workers were female, with 63 percent of them bookkeepers. Some professional groups were not as hospitable to women, for only 9 percent of accountants were women. Since 1910 there had been a continued polarization of work, with men having access to the higher-paid and more prestigious positions and women pushed into lower-level, clerical jobs. The new field of "personnel management" had emerged in recent years and women were seen particularly suited to this more "sensitive" and more "maternal" work. A new white-collar revolution was under way, benefiting women, even if it was at lower-paying jobs. During the hard economy of the 1930s, men's employment decreased 11 percent while women's increased 4 percent.

Partly because women were doing well at what they were allowed to do, the fears about them rose further in the Depression. According to a Gallup poll conducted in 1936, 82 percent of the population believed that a married woman should not work if her husband was employed. Such women were denounced as "thieving parasites." Women were pushed out of the economy, displaced by more "deserving" men, and when women did work, they suffered blatant wage discrimination, prompting them to organize themselves. A brassiere company office workers union began in 1937 and three years later led a strike wanting an "uplift in wages, because their company keeps them flatbusted" (as quoted in Boyer et al.'s *The Enduring Vision*).

My grandmother, Dorothy Stordock, was one of those "thieving parasites" who, despite having a husband, worked outside the home. Problem was Dorothy's husband Oscar—my maternal grandfather—was an alcoholic and could not support the family. Having a "drinking problem" was not the social scourge it is today and was, in fact, for some ethnic groups, quite normal male behavior. During the Depression, Dorothy worked at various jobs to support her five children, one of them with diabetes, while the oldest daughter, Katherine, would die from rheumatic fever during that decade. My grandmother used to talk mostly about her job as cook at Beloit College in Beloit, Wisconsin, where she was allowed to bring home food scraps in jars for her children to eat. Bedtimes were strict, because Dorothy had to spend the entire evening on housework. My own mother, Leone, had just one dress, which had to be washed and ironed each night.

My grandmother's life was difficult, with no love to keep her warm, not much of a sunny side of the street. As a young girl she may have dreamed about filling her man's desires, but as an adult, her hopes were few and far between. She may have wanted music to uplift her during the Depression, but there was not a lot of that either. They were so poor, they had no radio to listen to music.

WOMEN AND MUSIC

In the early days of the Depression, some of the top songs did not provide much of an escape, but rather added the melancholy longing of a Compliant yearning for unattainable love, as in two 1930 songs: one by Ruth Etting ("Ten Cents a Dance," no. 5) and the other from Helen Morgan ("Why Was I Born?" no. 8), plus one from 1931 by Libby Holman ("Love for Sale," no. 5) and another from 1938 by Mildred Bailey ("My Reverie," no. 10).

"TEN CENTS A DANCE"
Ten cents a dance, that's what they pay me.
Gosh, how they weigh me down.
Ten cents a dance, pansies and rough guys,
Tough guys who tear me down . . .

Sometimes I think I've found my hero.
But it's a queer romance.
All that you need is a ticket.
Come on, big boy, ten cents a dance!

Ruth Etting's song has a similarly jaded theme as the 1931 song below:

"LOVE FOR SALE"
Love for sale,
Appetizing young love for sale,
Love that's still fresh and unspoiled.
Love that's only slightly soiled . . .

"Innocent Sexpot Betty Boop and the Songs of the Depression"

If you want to buy my wares,
Follow me and climb the stairs.

So she's tired of selling herself to men and wants real love, but it proves illusive.

"My Reverie"
Our love
Is a dream, but in my reverie
I can see that this love was meant for me
Only a poor fool
Never schooled in the whirlpool
Of romance could be so cruel
As you are to me
My dreams are as worthless as tin to me
Without you life will never begin to be

If my only purpose in life is to sell my body for dances or other things and I cannot find true love, what's the point of living?

"Why Was I Born?" (later recorded by Billie Holiday)
Why was I born? Why am I living?
What do I get? What am I giving?
Why do I want a thing I daren't hope for?
Why do I try to draw you near me?
Why do I cry? You never hear me.
I'm a poor fool, but what can I do?
Why was I born to love you?

This theme continued throughout the decade. Similarly, Ethel Waters didn't want any responsibility when she declared "Don't Blame Me" (1933, no. 6) for falling in love with you, as your charms make me melt in your arms.

As we saw, in the first year of the Depression women's voice in song continued to be dependent and helpless. She wants the big hero, but all *he* wants is to spend a nickel to touch her and hold her body close to his. Then he's gone. She asks what's the purpose of life if all she does is cry for a man who doesn't even know she exists. She loved a man who was cruel to her and she considered her life worthless without his affection. It was the voice of a powerless woman and it sold lots of records. In fact, in the 1930s, codependency songs accounted for half of all female Top 40 songs.

Despite all the melancholy and negativity toward women's power, there were still girls listening to songs and records who got a positive message that carried them through adulthood. A real go-getter and trendsetter, Marilyn Winford didn't accept the message that she ought to be dependent, but rather held out hope in songs such as "Pennies from Heaven." She was more interested in what songs could do for her career, as she kept practicing and performing.

ℛEMINISCENCE

"Pennies From Heaven,"
Billie Holiday (with Teddy Wilson's Orchestra), 1937, no. 3

When I saw Loretta Young up on the screen in 1938 with David Niven in *Four Men and a Prayer*, I knew that moment my fate was sealed. I was nine years old and I wanted to be up on the screen, beautiful, just like she was. But the process of my career choice had actually begun a few months before, when my mother and father would sing "Pennies from Heaven" to me again and again.

It was the combination of that enchanted song and the movie that propelled me forth to what everyone else thought was a fairy tale dream. After all, we lived in Charleston, West

Virginia, and my father was a coal miner. My cousins used to make fun of me all the time, because I kept telling them I was going to leave those mountains and get to Hollywood. They kept calling me "Miss Hollywood."

But the end was in sight for me, and I would ask my father to pull out his guitar and play "Pennies from Heaven" for me, so I could practice it. My dream was to get on Charleston's radio "Farm Hour" and sing "Pennies from Heaven." We did, and I won a prize. That was the day that I knew for sure my future was in show business.

It took a lot of years and me being newly divorced and pregnant with my fifth child, but I got to Hollywood, starting my own acting workshop, which brought in some money. After my workshop got a good reputation, and I got other experience in show business, I went to the William Morris Agency in 1959 to persuade them to hire me as an artists' agent. Mind you, there were no women agents, managers, or executives back then in Hollywood. I was the first female agent in Hollywood. Later I went into writing and record producing. I'm seventy-two years old and still working in show business. I guess I did turn out to be "Miss Hollywood," and I can thank Loretta Young and "Pennies from Heaven."

Marilyn Winford, writer and producer
Los Angeles, California

Women's voice in music showed an eagerness to praise the male, that is, to build up his ego and make him think he is much better than her, as in the 1935 number-four Ethel Merman hit below:

"You're the Top"
You're the top! You're the Colosseum,
You're the top! You're the Louvre Museum . . .

I'm a worthless check, a total wreck, a flop,
But if, Baby, I'm the bottom,
You're the top!

The song actually goes on and on with many examples of how great he was and how worthless she was. But she loved it that way. In fact, in the movie where Ethel Merman sings that song, *Anything Goes* (with Bing Crosby, 1935), she delights in her gutter status. She actually wants to be an inferior? Compliant? It wasn't until 1937 that a hint of strength came from the woman's voice. Mildred Bailey's number-four hit "Trust in Me" sung of female stability (and was made a hit also in 1961 by Etta James).

"TRUST IN ME"
Trust in me in all you do
Have the faith I have in you
Love will see us through
If only you trust in me
Why don't you, you trust me

Come to me when things go wrong
Cling to me Daddy, oh yeah, and I'll be strong
We can get along, we can get along
Oh, if only you trust in me

At first glance "Trust in Me" seems like a breakthrough song in which the woman finally takes her place as a partner to her man. But on closer examination, what's there is a dependent woman still waiting for the man—in this case to trust her. So, until he does something (i.e., trust her), she is still powerless. And when he does trust her, the plan is not for equal partnership, but rather for her to be in charge. The idea of equal footing was so foreign back then that what we hear is that one or the other will be dominant and in control.

Billie Holiday was big during this era, recording hundreds of songs. Though many of the lyrics of her songs were not very different from other sentimental love songs, she sang them with a haunting clarity that captured the public's attention. She sang with deep emotion that captivated audiences because her life had been one pain after another. Growing up in a family made more unstable by racism, she never got enough love as a child. To make it worse, she was raped at age ten by a neighbor and was unjustly sent to a gruesome home for wayward girls for two years. It is no surprise that she ended up with self-destructive behavioral tendencies that ultimately led to her untimely death at age forty-four.

Billie Holiday's career was built in the thirties, continued strong in the forties, and through her records she reached many after her own death. For Billie, it was not only her lyrics but also her unique phrasing that has made her a legend. She sang from her heart. And she touched the hearts of many others, both young and old. Quite a number of her hits were sentimental love songs, but she had others, as well. "God Bless the Child" is about those that have, who get more, versus those that don't have, who get less; in other words, the injustice of extremes of wealth and poverty. It's a sad, compliant person observing the injustices of the world. At the same time, there is an underlying hopefulness for the child that God had blessed, so he doesn't have to worry about a thing. Because she came from a family that lived comfortably, Jennie Carter Thomas was able to relate to the positive part of the song.

ℛEMINISCENCE

"God Bless the Child," Billie Holiday, 1941, no. 25

I can't remember when I didn't know the song "God Bless the Child." Its sounds and words may even have taken root in my subconscious before I was born. When I was a little girl, my parents each had their own records. My father's were piano concertos, and my mother's were Rosemary Clooney, Sarah Vaughan, Billie Holiday, and a few Sinatras thrown in. Because my dad was an "electronics nut" and built most of our early record players and speakers, we always had great sound equipment—even in the late forties. My parents loved their music, and it was a big part of our lives.

My earliest real memory of the song was when I was around seven. We had just moved into a wonderful little house with a screened porch. It was a very hot summer that year, and my mom and I would lie on this large chaise lounge and listen to her music and read our books. Billie Holiday's voice would float across those hot afternoons. Sometimes we would hum or sing along. We had a yellow parakeet that my mother turned loose every afternoon on the porch so he could fly around. He would sing along, too. We would laugh and giggle at him. Then we would get all cleaned up and wait for my father to come home. His truck would come flying around the corner, and we would run out to meet him. Later he and Mother would dance around the living room to Mother's music. He taught me to dance that summer.

God has blessed this child from the beginning. My darling parents celebrated my life every day that they lived. They lit a special light within me. I can't remember when it wasn't there. Their love and inspiration gave me tremendous confidence and an optimistic outlook. I am also convinced it gave me a certain vision about my life that most young girls my age did not have at that time. All this made me independent and able to remake my life and persevere even in the terrible times of loss. I do have something that is truly my "own." It is that little light inside me.

A song often takes us back to another time, and "God

Bless the Child" certainly does that for me, but it does much more. It has an affirming message for me. It touches my identity. It reminds me that I have been "blessed" and that I can face what comes my way and make it through. The song always reminds me how much my parents loved me and how much they believed in me. Early on, I came to believe in myself, to like myself, to know it was okay to make mistakes as long as you took responsibility for them, and to know that there were tremendous opportunities for me and it was up to me to create my life.

The song has its personal message for me—whether I hear it at a Blood, Sweat and Tears concert, or hear Sarah Vaughan singing it at a little blues club in Georgetown, or play a Billie CD on my way to work. But truly, Billie sang it best. It was her song, too. Its message is my life. I have my "own," and God has blessed this child. Thank you Mother. Thank you Daddy. And thanks dear Billie—for giving me my song.

Jennie Carter Thomas, faculty member,
Belmont University,
NASHVILLE, TENNESSE

Billie Holiday's thirty-nine Top 40 songs included her singing that "I've Got My Love to Keep Me Warm" (1937, no. 4), but as poor as I am, "I Can't Give You Anything but Love" (1936, no. 5). She diverges from that in "I'm Gonna Lock My Heart" (1938, no. 2), where, as a rejected woman, she swears never to love anymore. A number of her songs were unique and even controversial. Most notable was her number-sixteen hit in 1939, "Strange Fruit," which was the first unmuted outcry against lynching and was even sung by an African-American woman. Unlike other songs, it provoked strong reactions, both of fright and of rage, and was banned from many radio stations.

"Strange Fruit"

Southern trees bear strange fruit,
Blood on the leaves and blood at the root,
Black bodies swinging in the southern breeze,
Strange fruit hanging from the poplar trees.
Pastoral scene of the gallant south,
The bulging eyes and the twisted mouth,
Scent of magnolias, sweet and fresh,
Then the sudden smell of burning flesh.
Here is fruit for the crows to pluck,
For the rain to gather, for the wind to suck,
For the sun to rot, for the trees to drop,
Here is a strange and bitter cry.

When Holiday sang the song, it was always the last in her set, as the emotion required for her to do it left her spent. Audiences were quiet, but it left them unsettled. It wasn't the typical song heard in clubs.

Billie Holiday was one of only three women vocalists in the first half of the century who were listed in VH1's *100 Greatest Women of Rock and Roll.* The other two were Bessie Smith and Ella Fitzgerald—all three African-Americans.

The end of the decade finally brought an innovation and some hope. The 1939 invention of nylon stockings by DuPont laboratories created a product to show off women's legs that would become an integral part of World War II folklore.

And Judy Garland won the lead role in *The Wizard of Oz,* taking on what was to become one of her signature songs, "Somewhere over the Rainbow" (1939, no. 5).

"Somewhere over the Rainbow"

Somewhere, over the rainbow, way up high,
There's a land that I heard of once in a lullaby.

Somewhere, over the rainbow, skies are blue,
And the dreams that you dare to dream really do come true.
Someday I'll wish upon a star
And wake up where the clouds are far behind me.
Where troubles melt like lemon drops
Away above the chimney tops
That's where you'll find me.
Somewhere over the rainbow, bluebirds fly,
Birds fly over the rainbow,
Why, then, oh why can't I?
If happy little bluebirds fly
Beyond the rainbow,
Why oh why can't I?

Finally, some strength. Or is it? Indeed, why oh why can't she fly beyond the rainbow? And yet, there is still the desire for dependency—for someone or something to take care of her problems. In this case, it is somewhere over the rainbow. If only she could be there, rather than here, well, her life would be just grand.

Judy Garland's lilty lyrics belied world politics. In that same year, Germany invaded Poland and occupied what is now the Czech Republic. Little did Americans realize that somewhere "over there" was about to come, sending millions of boys off to war. The running of the country, and much of the music, would be left to women, whose newfound independence would shatter many stereotypes at least for a short time.

SECOND MOVEMENT

Budding Strength Crushed into Compliance

VERSE THREE
1940-1949

"Patriotic and Powerful"

ARCHETYPES PRESENT:

Yearning/Jezebel

*P*atriotism resonated during this war-strewn decade. Music echoed women's prayers for men and their lingering codependency. Strong and smart women were perceived as scary, and materialistic women were simply gold-diggers. Women were yearning for their men and they were willing prisoners of their love.

What turned out to be a very hostile decade began with an unnoticed revolution. When the first network television was broadcast by NBC in 1941, little did an unsuspecting public sense what was to come. Movies were still supreme—for another decade or two, anyway. *Gone with the Wind* captured the American imagination when it hit the screens in 1940 and helped to numb the country to the bloodshed taking place across the oceans. Scarlett O'Hara was a feistier heroine than most, but she still needed southern feminine wiles to get her way.

Before the war started, women did not have many charted songs, and most of them were of the light and even silly kind. The Andrews

Sisters sang how they loved to "ride the ferry because the music is merry" ("Ferry Boat Serenade" 1940, no. 1) and told people to listen for that tick-a-tick-tick, in the "Woodpecker Song" (1940, no. 3). A song about Europe showed the American attempt to deny what was going on in the rest of the world. For while Hitler's armies invaded the Netherlands (home of Anne Frank) and the Final Solution was ordered, the King Sisters warbled "The Hut-Hut Song"(1941, no. 7), about a boy in Sweden who sat by the river listening to the song, which consisted mostly of nonsense syllables.

Judy Garland broke not only her own pattern from "Somewhere over the Rainbow," but she also veered away from the silly refrains, picking up the ain't-I-such-a-poor-lass songs heard frequently before. Her 1940 number-three hit "I'm Nobody's Baby" again brought the voice of a prisoner of love, displaying the lack of desire to function without a man.

"I'M NOBODY'S BABY"
I'm nobody's baby, I wonder why
Each night and day I pray the Lord above
Please send me down someone to love
But nobody wants me, I'm blue somehow. . . .

Around the same time, Dinah Shore lamented the loss of love from her "Jim" (1941, no. 5). He had taken her for granted, did not appreciate her nor show her love, yet she was unable to break free, as she shows in the end of the song:

"JIM"
Sometimes when I get feeling low,
I say, "Let's call it quits."
Then I hang on and let him go
Breaking my heart in bits.
Someday I know Jim will up and leave me,

But even if he does you can believe me,
I'll go on carrying the torch for Jim.

Pearl Harbor changed many things. Men went off to war and women were left behind to work in factories and offices. It didn't hurt women and music, for they were selling more records. As with World War I, patriotic songs arose, such as 1942's number-nine "The White Cliffs of Dover" by Kate Smith or "Praise the Lord and Pass the Ammunition" (by the male Kay Kyser, 1942, no. 1). Hollywood played it again, too, with *Casablanca,* a hopelessly romantic yet patriotic movie about Compliant sacrifice for ideals.

A number of songs in that year carried the loneliness theme, presumably for the boys over there. In 1942 the ever popular Andrews Sisters sang their number twenty-two tune "I'll Pray for You," because they were far, far apart, and Dinah Shore's number eight hit "I Miss You" lamented her lover's absence. Even the sultry Lena Horne sang her signature song, "Stormy Weather" (1943, no. 21) about how there's no sun in the sky and it's raining all the time since she and her man aren't together.

Yet there were also songs that were cheerful, trying to buoy up spirits with a "pollyanna-ish" lilt. Even though "You Are My Sunshine" was recorded by male singers in 1941, I always associated it with my mother singing it over and over again when I was a child. Below is a story of how a young girl was empowered to get through hard times by listening to the song.

*R*EMINISCENCE

"You Are My Sunshine," 1941, no. 19

The song that is my all-time favorite is "You Are My Sunshine." I think it is the first popular song that I learned and that was when I was in kindergarten—around

1942. My five-year-old neighbor had a new swing set. We were very poor and I could never imagine owning such a marvelous thing. She gave me permission to swing while she was on vacation. Every chance I got, I was on the swing, singing "You Are My Sunshine." The daisies and Queen Anne's lace in the field behind the swing were especially lovely when viewed from up above, as I stretched out flat and sailed as high in that swing as I possibly could go. Even now, if I hear that song, I see daisies and clear blue sky. When I think of it now, as an adult, that was the time that Mom was pregnant, Dad was called up in the draft, and things were really tense. Probably the song related very deeply in my young life to "please don't take my Daddy away," but all I really remember is the pure joy of sunshine on daisies and the exhilaration of lifting into space.

> *Winnie Merritt,*
> *Coordinator of the Agricultural Forum*
> MOUNT AIRY, NORTH CAROLINA

Most of the songs by women in those war years were full of yearning—gushy love, "Gobs of Love," crooning about a "Dearly Beloved" who had been sent from heaven asking a "Skylark" where her love is, and Kate Smith wondering "How Do I Know It's Real?" Two exceptions were by Dinah Shore and the Andrews Sisters and they both spoke of stronger Wonder Women, influenced by the sense of power women were experiencing now that men were off fighting.

Dinah sang her you-done-me-wrong song "Blues in the Night" (1942, no. 4), a song also recorded by other singers. It was a refreshing counterpoint to the sappy songs of those years and owes its theme and style to the early African-American women blues singers such as Ma Rainey and Bessie Smith. Finally the impact of the more realistic blues music became more prevalent in the Top 40. Here was somebody telling it like it was, not like it ought to be.

"Blues in the Night"
My momma done told me
When I was in pigtails
My momma done told me, hon
A man's gonna sweet-talk
And give you the glad eye
But when that sweet-talkin's done
A man is a two-faced, a worrisome thing
Who'll leave you to sing the blues in the night

Another exception to the schmaltzy tunes was the Andrews Sisters number-two 1943 "Pistol-Packin' Mama," written by hillbilly star Al Dexter and purportedly patterned after the raucous and proud Appalachian coal miner's daughter, Aunt Molly Jackson—singer and social activist—who was discovered and brought north, but never gave up her offensive and self-involved ways.

"Pistol Packin' Mama"
Lay that pistol down, Babe,
Lay that pistol down.
Pistol Packin' Mama,
Lay that pistol down.

Oh, she kicked out my windshield
And she hit me over the head.
She cussed and cried and said I lied
And she wished that I was dead . . .

We're three tough gals
From deep down Texas way.
We got no pals
They don't like the way we play.
We're a rough rootin', tootin', shootin' trio

47

But you ought to see my sister Cleo
She's a terror make no error
But there ain't no nicer terror
Here's what we tell her:

Lay that pistol down, Babe.
Lay that pistol down.
Pistol packin' mama
Lay that pistol down . . .

Here again is the dichotomy between the sweet and lovely, dependent and needy female and the aggressive, murderous female. The hunger for the nasty side of women was shown by the song's number-two ranking and record sales of over 1 million copies, which was a lot back then, earning it a gold record. That dichotomy was further fueled by two images of wartime women: one was the strong and dependable Rosie the Riveter, who, despite her bulging arm muscles, has an attractive face, so we can assume she uses makeup and cares for her appearance. She is Wonder Woman on the surface, but really yearns to be a prisoner of love. The other icon capturing attention during that era was the charming but deceitful Tokyo Rose, who was seen as the Jezebel Delilah, ready to bring the downfall of otherwise good and decent men, in this case those sacrificing and patriotic soldiers stationed in the Pacific.

The year 1943 was a slump year for women's music, which rated only one out of twenty-five of all charted songs. But the main reason the music "died" was the American Federation of Musicians ban on recording, which began in August of 1942. The dispute over musicians' royalties was settled with the record companies in 1944, but by that time the landscape had changed and vocalists had regained their place in music center-stage, as they had before the big bands and swing era took over in the 1930s.

It was an unusual time historically. Women were in the workplace in record numbers, proving they could do a job for a woman—or a man, such as welding or machine tooling. Because 12 million men were in the armed forces, there was great need for females to take over a multitude of jobs. Minority women were not so lucky to get the higher-paying factory jobs. Over half of them were still domestic maids. Over 6 million women entered the workforce in the early forties, an increase of almost 50 percent. It was the first time that married working women outnumbered single women.

After the war had been going on for a couple of years, the pressure was mounting to integrate these *girls* into the male workaday world. The best example I have found that shows the patronizing attitude toward women was in a 1943 issue of *Mass Transportation* (as reprinted in the fall 1999 issue of *Woman and Language*), containing an article, which really wanted to be helpful to perplexed employers. Its eleven tips for getting more efficiency out of women workers included: (1) hire young married women, who are more responsible and less flirtatious than those unmarried; (2) "husky" girls are more reliable than their underweight sisters; (3) have a physician give physical examinations to determine if any of the women have female conditions that would make them physically or mentally unfit for the work; (4) define their workday and tasks very carefully, as females tend to have difficulty planning their own work or taking initiative; and (5) every girl should be given enough breaks during the day to tidy her hair, as well as apply lipstick and makeup, because that keeps them happier.

But there was another kind of working woman. Rosie the Riveter was a real person named Betty Murphy who worked at the Douglas aircraft factory in the Los Angeles area (chronicled by historian Sherna Gluck). Formerly a waitress, Murphy took on the higher-paid riveting work during the war. She soon realized that Douglas did not pay the same overtime and benefits as other employers, and that managers at Douglas had too much power over young female subordinates. Secretly working toward unionization, Murphy believed that unions would protect women. Because of the work of women such as Murphy, the Equal Pay Act was introduced to the U.S. Congress in 1945, but it did not pass. Murphy was successful enough, though, to become a union official and was one of the lucky few to hold her job after the war, when almost 5 million women left the labor force within a year.

As the prospects of peace rose, prominent women took up the call to remind women that they belonged back in the home, taking care of families. Two remarkably independent women, Eleanor Roosevelt and Margaret Mead, led the charge to restore women to their rightful places in society, namely as wives and mothers.

Toward the beginning of 1945, as the war was winding down and women were getting used to more responsibility back in the home, a new song hit the charts. It must have captured the deep sentiments of women, who no doubt knew that when the men came back their lives would return to servitude. "Don't Fence Me In" (Andrews Sisters, no. 1, and Kate Smith, no. 8) is often today associated with the male need for independence, fueled by its cowboy imagery. But judging by the popularity of this song, sung by women in the mid-forties, it is more likely to have been an anthem for women desiring their freedom to continue. The independent side of women was peeping through, albeit briefly.

"Don't Fence Me In"
Don't fence me in
Just give me land, lots of land, under starry skies above,
Don't fence me in.
Let me ride through the wide-open country that I love,
Don't fence me in!

A similar theme was sung by Judy Garland in the 1945 number-ten song "On the Atchison, Topeka, and the Santa Fe," which spoke longingly about travel and seeing new places, about the thrill of new views from the train. Women wanted more space, more opportunity, not less as was coming down the pike. A few years after the war, the themes were quite different. Compare "Don't Fence Me In" with Dinah Shore's 1948 number one hit, the Compliant "Buttons and Bows," which demands she live in confined spaces, where "cement grows" and where women wear "buttons and bows."

The war ended. Good for the world, not great for the cause of women's equality. Men wanted their jobs back. And gone were the top-selling songs about men being two-faced, or women wanting freedom. Instead, 1946 brought not only the mass production of jukeboxes, but also women singing about being stupid, such as in Dinah Shore's number-three hit "Doin' What Comes Naturally" (from the Broadway show *Annie Get Your Gun,* discussed below), which told us that girls didn't need to be able to read or write in order to be out with their fella. Dinah Shore's 1946 number-ten song "Personality" also stated that women's intelligence or skills were not important, but wiles and charms were. Shore sings how a girl doesn't have to be a good speller or even know dictation to catch the boss's eye. All she really needs is a good "personality."

Postwar reactions to female wartime strength included the successful but man-eating (and pitiful mother) Joan Crawford as the title character in *Mildred Pierce* and the Broadway hit *Annie Get Your Gun.* One of the themes of the latter (as staged in 1946, not necessarily in the 1999 revival) was how ridiculous a woman looks when she tries to do things that only men should do. In other words, it is more natural for females to be soft and gentle. Annie Oakley was portrayed as a pitiful excuse for a woman, one who was acting too much like a man and, as a result, was unattractive and unappealing to men. One of Annie's goals, before she sees the light, is to beat Frank Butler at shooting. The sense of competition intensifies with the song "Anything You Can Do, I Can Do Better," where Annie and Frank argue about who can do things better.

The *real* story, of Annie and Frank, as told by Gerri Gribi, is more about women's opportunity and a marriage of equals than the Broadway play depicted. The young and accomplished markswoman Annie turned up at a contest that traveling champion sharpshooter Frank Butler arranged near her home in Cincinnati in 1881. The undefeated champion reportedly laughed when he saw this skinny, five foot short, fifteen-year-old opponent. But the confident Annie beat him and won not only the hundred-dollar prize but also Frank's heart. They were married the following year and began a career together as sharpshooters. After a few years, Frank retired from shooting and became his wife's manager, and their marriage was evidently strong, with Frank continuing to write love poems to his wife throughout the years. The role of the supportive husband to a strong woman rested well with this masculine sharpshooter. When Annie died in 1926, as a result of injuries from an earlier auto accident, Frank lived only a few days longer. People said he died of a broken heart.

Why the distortion of a really good and touching story of love and marriage? In the late 1940s women had to leave their desired jobs to make room for the men returning from war. It was not a willing exit. A Women's Bureau study in 1944 showed that 80 percent of women needed or at least preferred to stay in the paid workforce. Secretary of Labor Frances Perkins (the first-ever woman cabinet member) urged companies to keep women workers after the war. President Harry Truman did not support her wishes, though, and did nothing in 1946 as large corporations instituted blanket firings of married women.

None of that stopped young Josephine Esther Mentzer, who took her chemist uncle's formulas in 1948 and, with her unusual business acumen, built them into what is today a billion-dollar empire of the women's cosmetics line, Estée Lauder.

Other forces were at work, too. Was it a conscious onslaught of media against the "selfish" women who would deny their families the time and attention they thought they deserved from wives and mothers? I don't think there was any large conspiracy of newspapers, songwriters, and media. But the aching needs of men to be gainfully employed spoke louder in the "culture war" than women's needs to stay in the workforce. Helping this along was the 1948 recession, whose threats were exaggerated beyond reason by a Depression-weary nation. There was a period of more than ten years in the United States filled with movies, books, magazine articles, and songs depicting the ideal woman as compliant and passive.

The end of World War II had the opposite effect in some Asian countries. China was moving into the twentieth century by abolishing its feudal system and officially giving women equality with men, while Japan's and India's new constitutions gave women the right to vote. Within a few years India also outlawed polygamy.

Back in Top 40, a musical theme that was to appear in coming years was that of woman-as-gold-digger. This was no doubt partly a result of women being relegated back to a state of dependency. Because you must rely on someone else for your upkeep, it makes sense to find someone on whom you can truly depend economically. No one talked about the materialism of women being borne out of their renewed dependency. Rather, it was a sign of a mean and evil woman, as sung in the Andrews Sisters number-seven hit in 1947.

"THE LADY FROM 29 PALMS"
She left twenty-nine broken hearts
Broken in 29 parts
Now there are twenty-nine fellas complainin' to their moms
About the lady from 29 Palms.

She got twenty-nine Cadillacs
Twenty-nine sables from Saks
They came from twenty-nine fellas
Who never had their arms
Around the lady from 29 Palms.

At the end of the decade, the compliant prisoner of love theme returned, and *South Pacific* became the number-one *Billboard* album for an astounding sixty-nine weeks. Two of the songs were rerecorded and became top hits. "Some Enchanted Evening" became a number-four hit for Jo Stafford in that year, while Margaret Whiting scored at number twelve with "A Wonderful Guy," which raved about the wonderful guy she was in love with. Another enduring song from that show that did not hit the charts was "I'm Gonna Wash That Man Right Outa My Hair." Though that song is still remembered well today, the message of kicking a man out when he doesn't behave perhaps prevented it from making the charts. Being rebellious was not as popular as loving *a wonderful guy.*

One song that rose above many of the sentimental love songs in those last years of the 1940s was the 1949 "That Lucky Old Sun," which became a hit for six artists that year, including Sarah Vaughan (no. 14). It was about the toils of life and how that lucky old sun had nothing to do but roll around in heaven all the day. Then she asks the sun to send the silver-lined cloud and lift her to paradise and wash her troubles away. It is a woman asking for help, for fate—or the sun in this case—to make her life better. A young girl, who had no choice but be dependent, listened to the song and it helped her through hard times.

ℛEMINISCENCE

"That Lucky Old Sun," 1949, no. 14

I clung to the words of the song. They kept me up when I was down and became some of the glue that held me together during difficult times in my home life as a young girl. In 1949, I was ten years old and my mother had died when I was barely six years old. "That Lucky Old Sun" was a poignant piece. It let me know that I wasn't the only one with troubles and sadness. I dragged through those days, and, frankly, I'm glad they're over. As a ten-year-old girl, I didn't have the resources that I have today. "That Lucky Old Sun" stands out in my memory as a tune that resonated with my feelings at that time. I'll never forget it.

Diann Stevens
Sacramento, California

The last few years before the fifties were momentous and too much was going on to pay much attention to women's issues: The birth of the U.N., independence in India, the cultural revolution in China, and the division of Germany. Women's concerns seemed trivial in the face of all this worldwide drama. Not much notice was given to the fact that women didn't take to their postwar retirings. Even with the husbands back home and working, the families needed her earnings. By 1947, women started going back to work and within a year, married women once again outnumbered single women in the workplace. This happened despite the common practice of firing any woman once she became pregnant. And while men's wages rose dramatically, those of women increased by only half as much. It would take more than a decade before women could be heard—before their voices were given some respect, both in the workplace and in song.

VERSE FOUR
1950s—MID-1960s

"Rigid Gender Roles and Blissful Compliance"

ARCHETYPES PRESENT:
Compliant/Jezebel

*M*usic in the 1950s and mid-1960s rang out with rigid gender roles—girls were girls and they wanted cavemen for boys. Women loved their men even if they treated them like dirt. Codependence was back in full force. The archetypes for this period were either the suppliant, compliant wife or the cruel-hearted Jezebel.

Two great thefts occurred as this decade began. In January 1950, the infamous Brink's robbery shocked the nation. The other theft was quieter, more subtle: Women's self-esteem, which had shown its head in the early 1940s, was repressed during this whole "silent generation" era. Furthermore, the apparent conformity of women was ironic, considering that 1957 was the year that women began to vote in the same proportions as men.

Doris Day's number nine 1950 hit "Bewitched" captured the spirit of the ideal and childlike compliant women in society, with these lines:

"BEWITCHED"
I'm wild again, beguiled again
A simpering, whimpering child again
Bewitched, bothered, and bewildered am I

The song then goes on to chronicle how much she loves it when he mistreats her:

He is cold, I agree
He can laugh but I love it
Although the laugh's on me
I'll sing to him, each Spring to him
And long for the day when I cling to him

The fact that seven competing versions of this song made the Top 40 is a strong indication that these lyrics reflected some belief in society. Be a simpering child. He is cold. That's how men are. Just laugh when he mistreats you. These ideas sold a lot of records.

Such beliefs not only disempower women, but to a large extent they also stereotype men. This song indicates that most men are cads and creeps. It's just that poor, weak dependent women did not have the strength to withstand his advances. In fact, the Andrews Sisters number-one hit from 1950, "I Wanna Be Loved," sings of how she wants to be passively swept off her feet in love, with inspiration and sensation, without conversation, because she is in "no mood to resist." Talk about being compliant and giving up her power!

When I think of these songs and those of the forties, all I have to do is compare my grandmother and mother. My grandmother threw out her alcoholic husband (my grandfather), even though she had five children to support on her own. She was strong, and that strength was supported by the power of women during World War II. Then came my mother, who lived with a battering husband for many years. But my mother stayed with him no matter what, seemingly forgiving him—just as all those songs told her to, until she finally left him after eighteen years. There was not much in the culture of the fifties that would support her standing up to him and finding her own strength: No matter what he does, you have to forgive him.

Another topic that appeared in songs was jealousy between women—over men. Later on, as women gained more of a sense of power in their music, there were fewer songs about jealousy toward other women. But in this Compliant era, the currency of male love was highly important, because it was the meal ticket and often the chance for higher status. Hence the great threat women posed to one another regarding their men, as shown by the story below.

$\mathscr{R}$EMINISCENCE

"Tennessee Waltz," Patti Page, 1950, no. 1

Though my parents divorced when I was five, and my father remarried shortly after the divorce, I never thought that his new wife had anything to do with the divorce. But when I was eight, my mother began dating a man named Tracy, who treated me very kindly and always took me along when they went out to dinner. I recall them taking me to a roadhouse one night where there were little boxes at each table, which allowed you to select a song from the jukebox. I loved these. Tracy gave me many dimes with which to select the music, and I was paying attention to the music; the song playing was the "Tennessee Waltz." I listened very carefully to the words, and when I heard the lyric: "and while they were dancing, my friend stole my sweetheart from me," I was first aware that two women could actually be in competition for a man. Why that had never occurred to me before that I don't know, but it made a deep impression on me. My experience with women was that they were extremely cooperative and mutually supporting in the face of difficulties. I was amazed that a woman could actually be the source of betrayal in a friendship. Reflecting back, I realize that I knew that men could be jerks, but it had never occurred to me that women could be cruel as well. It was a revelation to me, and I suddenly regarded my stepmother, who had treated me coolly, in a new light.

> *Mary K. Radpour,*
> *licensed clinical social worker*
> CHATTANOOGA, TENNESSEE

The messages that resonated with the larger population were not only of compliance and passivity, but also of women as blissful domestic engineer. Eileen Barton also hit number one in 1950 with her song about what the ideal woman does. "If I Knew You Were Comin' I'd've Baked a Cake" chronicled a woman, evidently sitting at home doing domestic chores (we don't usually picture her running a home-based business) when a friend unexpectedly drops in. Our woman is apologetic for not having prepared a grand welcome. The fact that four competing versions of this song hit the Top 40 once again shows how closely this image reflected the way in which the culture viewed women. Similarly, in 1951, Rosemary Clooney's number-one hit "Come On-A My House" was all about taking someone home and feeding him, one of a woman's main roles.

Another force to sweep American society, and which no doubt impacted the music industry, was McCarthyism. Joseph McCarthy, the senator from my home state of Wisconsin, captured national attention in 1950 with his allegation that 205 Communists had managed to infiltrate the U.S. State Department. His hearings and subsequent blacklisting of writers and artists sent shock waves through the entertainment industry, forcing them to avoid controversial topics for the rest of the decade.

The postwar desire for ultrafeminine women combined with the fears of McCarthyism and resulted in bland fare in music. The 1950s brought First Lady Mamie Eisenhower, a dependent and sweet woman you might want as your grandmother, but not exactly a rebel to lead the charge for independence, as well as vapid songs such as "How Much Is That Doggie in the Window?" (Patti Page, 1953, no. 1), "The Aba Daba Honeymoon" (Debbie Reynolds, 1951, no. 3), and "Botch-A-Me" (Rosemary Clooney, 1952, no. 2). Some might say that women purposefully initiated a sense of playfulness in music. If you can't speak the truth, another way to have some power is through the humor. There were also cute and folksy tunes, such as "A Bushel and a Peck," recorded by a number of artists in 1950, including the Andrews Sisters (no. 22), Margaret Whiting (with Jimmy Wakely, no. 6), Betty Hutton (with Perry Como, no. 3), and Doris Day. In fact, the power of humor in this upbeat song was an inspiration for a young mother.

ℛEMINISCENCE

"A Bushel and a Peck," Doris Day, 1950 no. 16

Doris Day sang, "I love you, a bushel and a peck" when I was a little girl but it stayed in my mind because I enjoyed its spirit and lyric simplicity. I also enjoyed the vernacular, or dialect, perhaps because I'm from West Virginia. When my son was born and I held him in my arms, nursing him while rocking slowly in a chair, I sang that wonderfully direct and loving song to him. Also at bedtime, I sang that song to him slowly, with gentle and soft tones, like a lullaby. As an adult, he remembers those times, and during a recent visit to me with his wife he had me sing as he went to bed how I loved him "a bushel and a peck . . ." And I bet his pretty neck that I do!

Lynda Tae Reed, artist and writer
CHARLESTON, WEST VIRGINIA

Compliance was everywhere in the 1950s and even went beyond women's issues. One of the current design innovations of the century was invented by Charles and Ray Eames (married couple), and it epitomized the spirit of the age: compliant and without definable shape. They introduced the classic fiberglass side-shell chair, the ones that look sleek but are a chiropractor's nightmare. These are the chairs that allow the spine to bend almost without shape—to conform and comply, as the sitter slides farther down on the slippery slope. Much of the furniture designed in the 1950s had that minimalist, stark, and uncozy look that characterized that lackluster decade.

Doris Day's 1952 number-one "A Guy Is a Guy" is a song about a young man who follows a girl home. Though they have never met, he even goes to her door and kisses her. All the time she knows he is there and what he will do (because a guy is a guy, after all), wanting him to pursue her, but never letting on. It almost sounds like he is stalking her, but in this case she loves it. Isn't that what men have been saying all along? That women might say "no," but they really mean "yes." Those guys must have listened to too many Top 40 songs and that's where they got the idea.

Also in 1952, Joni James's number-one hit "Why Don't You Believe Me?" criticized the man for not trusting her, while another number-one song, Georgia Gibbs's "Kiss of Fire," willingly gave her over as a "slave," but cautioned the listener not to pity her. She *wanted* to be dominated.

We can't talk about the fifties and compliance or domination without mentioning a popular series of movies, beginning in 1959, about a petite and perky but dependent young woman named Gidget, originally played by Sandra Dee. Another one of the most popular movies and its theme song from 1957, *Tammy,* starred Debbie Reynolds. A young, uneducated backwoods girl ends up going to civilization and winning the heart of an older, educated, and wealthy man, played by Leslie Nielsen (way before he became identified with the *Airplane* movies). The song is sung with a sweet and innocent voice. He is her superior in every way: height, age, education, and finances. But she is shown to be better than him in common sense and folk wisdom. It harks back to Dinah Shore's 1946 song about how folks are dumb and uneducated but able to be successful in life by just acting naturally.

A compliant teenager falling in love with an older man was not an uncommon theme in movies in the late forties and fifties. *The Bachelor and the Bobby Soxer* (1947, starring Cary Grant, Myrna Loy, and a teenage-like Shirley Temple); *Sabrina* (1954, starring Humphrey Bogart, William Holden, and Audrey Hepburn); *Susan Slept Here* (1954, with Dick Powell and Debbie Reynolds); and *Gigi* (1958, starring Louis Jourdan and Leslie Caron). Literature, too, was fascinated with this topic, as evidenced by the attention given to Vladimir Nabokov's 1955 novel *Lolita*, about the scandalous affair between a middle-aged man and his twelve-year-old step-daughter.

If women were the young ones in the relationship, that made for light comedy or heartwarming drama. When the man is older and richer, he is all the more attractive to the nubile and lovable female. But turn the tables so that the woman is the older partner and suddenly we are in psychoville, inhabited by needy, desperate women and gutter-crawling men. Consider *Sunset Boulevard*, one of the biggest movies of 1950, with former silent movie star Gloria Swanson playing fifty-year-old faded actress Norma Desmond. She had enough wealth to seduce struggling writer William Holden, who nonetheless hated himself for becoming a sex object. The 1961 hit, *The Roman Spring of Mrs. Stone*, portrayed Vivien Leigh as the faded star, the older and wealthier woman who was pitiful and needed to pay a despicable man to love her. In coming years, the younger-female phenomenon was chronicled in Steve Lawrence's "Go Away Little Girl" (1963, no. 1) and Gilbert O'Sullivan's "Claire" (1972, no. 2), where he can barely keep his hands off the girl he is supposed to be baby-sitting. But equal attention and respect was not given to the older woman–younger man scenario.

Television echoed the dependent and compliant characteristics in five of the most popular TV shows of the decade: *Ozzie and Harriet, Leave It to Beaver, The Donna Reed Show, Make Room for Daddy,* and *Father Knows Best.* In each case, the following were the norms: the mother, always cheery and doting, and crisply attired in starched dress and apron, prepared elaborate dinners and hearty, packed lunches. Interestingly, they all looked as if they might be sisters, with medium-to-dark hair, average build and height, and similar accents. Though they might not be hired in today's sitcom world due to their lack of an anorexic look, they epitomized the ideal woman of the fifties: happy (with no hint of PMS or menopause), hardworking, and solely focused on family caretaking.

Another show took a slightly different approach. Lucille Ball coproduced *I Love Lucy* with her husband, Desi Arnaz. When the show premiered in 1951, it showed a ditsy Lucy, always scheming with her neighbor Ethel Mertz to fool their husbands and get some reward: whether a chance to be in Ricky's show, to meet some important people, or to help someone. Rather than being only domestically focused, Lucy always had some other agenda. In other words, she was ambitious and not very Compliant, but the culture of the fifties did not allow her aspirations to reach very high. She was "just a girl." Hence the ditsy and fun Lucy who won the hearts of America. Ball's persona hid the business genius that lay beneath, and she became one of the most powerful women in the new medium of television.

During this era, girls were girls (and dependent ones, at that) and boys were boys. This was partly a result of all those guys dreaming for several years during the war about their sweethearts back home, and imagining how wonderfully feminine they would be. Toward the end of this overly needy Compliant era came a song from Broadway telling all of us what we should be like. Rodgers and Hammerstein's *Flower Drum Song* had one truly memorable tune, "I Enjoy Being a

Girl," about a gal who loves lace dresses, swoons when a guy brings her flowers, chats endlessly on the phone, and longs for a brave male who'll take care of her.

And wasn't that what we all dreamed about? A handsome and rich guy who would sweep us off our feet and take care of us, happily ever after? What were our career goals back then? To be a wife and mother, mostly. Even though I knew I had to support myself, as I came from a long line of women as breadwinners I secretly still wanted Prince Charming to rescue me from myself. And if you didn't want to be a housewife but rather wanted to have a career, what were the role models? *The Flying Nun,* starring Sally Field, which premiered in 1967, showing a woman with a little more ambition but enclosed in a confining nun's habit and pointy hat.

Doris Day sometimes portrayed a career woman, but one who was waiting for her Prince Charming. In *Pillow Talk* (1959), *That Touch of Mink* (1962), and *Lover Come Back* (1961) she was an innocent and Compliant woman looking for a brave guy. In these movies, she wasn't Compliant enough to give in to him sexually, for that would have made her a slut. And, she retained her virginity and her self-righteousness, because she became indignant if he would even ask her to do it. She remained beautiful and desirable by saying no at the right time.

One of my favorite songs from that era comes from an Alfred Hitchcock movie, *The Man Who Knew Too Much.* Turns out this song is a favorite of a lot of people. As I have toured the world doing performances of this program—excerpts of songs showing the voice of women in popular music—the song that audiences sing along with the most and with extra gusto is Doris Day's number-two hit in 1956, "Que Sera, Sera." As I sing the song and look out at the audiences of hundreds, people link arms and sway back and forth. And how beautifully the lyrics describe the state of mind of the ideal woman in that era. Her role was to ask everyone else what she should be or do. She didn't take responsibility for her own destiny, instead giving up her power to those around her. We call this *external locus of control.* Never would it occur to her to have her own dreams, her own goals, her own plans.

"Que Sera, Sera"
When I grew up and fell in love
I asked my sweetheart
What lies ahead
Will we have rainbows?
Day after day?
Here's what my sweetheart said
Que sera, sera
Whatever will be, will be
The future's not ours to see
Que sera, sera
What will be, will be

The downside of rigid gender roles was that young and feminine women grew into old hags. When you depend on beauty for your identity, what happens when beauty fades? It's pretty scary if you believed Hollywood back then. Just a couple of years after the success of "I Enjoy Being a Girl" came two blockbuster movies that showed, all too graphically, the fate of young women who lived to please men. Bette Davis and Joan Crawford played the aging and grossly ugly Jezebel film stars who verged on mental illness in 1962's *What Ever Happened to Baby Jane?* Its success led to a similar film in 1964 with Bette Davis once again caricatured as the faded beauty in *Hush, Hush Sweet Charlotte* (whose title song by Patti Page went to number eight in 1965).

When I was young, none of that registered consciously with me. Because of where I am now, I know I was paying attention to more positive role models. As I look back on it, one of the earliest media influences suggesting girls could be something all their own was, surprisingly, my favorite fifties TV show: *The Mickey Mouse Club*. Every day I watched as Annette (she was the best, as far as I was concerned), Darlene, and Karen entranced me with their singing and dancing. They were every bit as good as the boys and got to do the same stuff as the guys. Unlike other TV shows where the girl wore confining dresses and had limited activities, the Mouseketeers gave equal status to the females. That show gave me the first real hope that my life could be something other than what it was. It offered me a dream to get away from Woodland Drive in Pewaukee, Wisconsin. But not everyone around me believed I could ever escape that place.

One of those people was the mother of my friend Nancy Stramka (I have disguised her real name). She lived one street up in what seemed a pretty swell house, though now I realize it was small and plain. Her father worked every day and evidently brought home a paycheck, because Mrs. Stramka did not work outside the home. In fact, the only time she ever left the house, as far as I could tell, was to go grocery shopping and to church. They were pretty ordinary people, basically decent, and Nancy's mother was what they used to call "a good housekeeper." I used to think of the poem about Jack Sprat and his wife when I went there, for Mrs. Stramka was very, very heavy and her husband was very, very thin.

One day Nancy and I were sitting in front of her TV watching *The Mickey Mouse Club*, and I was gazing adoringly at Annette and Karen, mentioning that someday I wanted to be there. Mrs. Stramka, who was sitting beside us on her plastic-covered aqua-blue rectangular couch, looked straight at me and in her most serious I-am-going-to-let-you-down-easily voice, the kind that tries to cover up the intense condescension, said,

"Dorothy, you have to have *talent* to be on that show."

For some people that might have been the hand that slaps you down. But that one sentence of Mrs. Stramka's became a rallying point for me over the years. Whenever my life got difficult and I thought I couldn't make it, all I had to do was remember Mrs. Stramka looking at me with disdain. Was I going to let Mrs. Stramka be right, or was I going to follow Annette's lead? There was never any doubt in my mind which one was the right path.

Why were women this needy and dependent? Because they were still beholden to men economically. Less than one-third of all women were in the paid labor force, and three-quarters of married women were completely dependent on their husbands. Those who did work earned little. The fifties saw an increase of 3 million working women in the clerical and service sectors but this was partly attributable to the new advertising-driven consumer society, which demanded more money to purchase the new material "necessities."

Back in the mid-fifties no one thought anything about having newspaper ads in separate categories: jobs for women, jobs for men. How could women be much of anything *except* dependent? Even women, like my mother, who did work were often without many choices. With her limited education, she supported us by being a waitress and a school-bus driver, both with limited earnings.

The smart thing for a hopelessly dependent person to do would be to ensure that whomever she was going to be dependent on would themselves be economically sufficient. Hence the era of the gold-digger woman, or, at minimum, the perception of that kind of woman. How many movies portrayed women as searching out the richest man? *How to Marry a Millionaire* and *Gentlemen Prefer Blondes* (both from 1953) are good examples. This ethos is embodied in one of the songs from the latter movie. The song also includes a bit of Jezebel.

"Diamonds Are a Girl's Best Friend"
A kiss on the hand may be quite continental
But diamonds are a girl's best friend
A kiss may be grand but it won't pay the rental
On your humble flat or help you at the automat
Men grown cold as girls grow old
And we all lose our charms in the end

But square cut or pear-shaped
These rocks don't lose their shape
Diamonds are a girl's best friend

Four years later, in 1957, a number twenty-five hit that is now for-gotten had a similar theme: Ruth Brown's "Lucky Lips," about a not very good-looking woman who knows she won't have to worry, she'll have diamond clips, because she has lucky lips!

On the other hand, 1957 also brought an anti-gold-digger song from Patti Page. "A Poor Man's Roses" hit number twelve and told of how the poor man's rose of love means more to her than any gold of a rich man. The focus on money reflected the growing prosperity of Americans, or else a growing need of materialistic pleasures. Since the end of the Second World War, gross national product had doubled and the inflation-adjusted average family income had increased 50 percent in just one decade.

That same song—"A Poor Man's Roses"—was first recorded by country star Patsy Cline in 1956, but Patsy did not have the crossover power back then to bring that song to the charts, as Patti Page did the following year. Patsy did have a hit that year, "Walkin' after Mid-night," which hit number twelve, and she had a string of other crossover hits in the following few years ("Crazy," no. 9, and "I Fall to Pieces," no. 12, both in 1961; "She's Got You," no. 14 in 1962) until her untimely death in an airplane crash in 1963.

In the midst of all the 1950's codependence, a few glimmers of strength showed through. Teresa Brewer's 1952 "Gonna Get Along without You" (no. 25) chronicles a relationship in which she loves him more than he loves her, he plays around, and she gives him her money and sacrifices her pride, but finally she wakes up and says good-bye. Patience and Prudence did a slightly modified version of that song in 1956, which got to number eleven (they also charted number four with "Tonight You Belong to Me," but we never heard from them again). Even though there was some anger in the words, these eleven- and fourteen-year-old sisters sang it with an innocent sweetness that belied the meaning. They also changed the words slightly so that it is not clear whether she broke up with him or he left her first. Brewer's 1952 version was more mature and more angry. It's not surprising that Brewer's version only made number twenty-five, while "A Guy Is a Guy" (about the stalker) and "Half as Much" (seeking codependence) both made number one in that same year.

A compliant song with some inner strength appeared in 1957 and hit the charts later in 1964. While "I Wish You Love" was about the heartbreak of lost love, power comes from her voice when she says that she will be the one to set him free. She has enough inner resources to send him off with hopes for love and not begrudge his happiness. Marcia Day is reminded of her late ex-husband's love when she hears that song.

*R*EMINISCENCE

"I Wish You Love,"
Keely Smith, 1957; and Gloria Lynne, 1964, no. 28

There is one very special song that often invades my mind. Without thought, in the bathtub, the kitchen sink, or in the car. I can hear myself singing the words about shelter in the story, a fire to keep cozy-warm, and while the snowflakes fall, I do wish you love. Even though my aching heart knows that we could never be, I set you free with my very best.

That was the song my husband sang to me at a lovely candlelight dinner on the evening of our divorce, in Hollywood of 1958, after recently celebrating my thirtieth birthday. I sat there grieving for the end of my fourteen-year marriage to a man I had loved and adored for most of those years.

By then my heart had frozen from the pain and struggle of trying to raise five daughters at such a young age, all the while doing my best to be wife, friend, lover, sister, and, yes, at times the family provider. To save my children and my sanity I had no other choice but set him free. Those were my thoughts during that evening. When dinner was over, we walked hand in hand to the piano and behind his tears he somehow managed to get through the song, "I Wish You Love."

I often wonder if this song enabled him to keep his promise, a promise he made to me on his death from alcohol disease in 1989 in his daughter's apartment. No way were his five daughters going to let him die alone in a Veteran's Administration hospital. Those five days in that small apartment made up for a life together. All the despair was replaced with laughter and tears of joy. The bonding and love between father and daughters brought such joy to my heart as I, too, witnessed it there.

In his last moments, we gathered around. My face was the last thing he saw before he left this world, as he told me, "I couldn't help you and the girls. If there is any way in the next world to reach you, to help you, I promise, I promise. Please forgive me. I wish you love."

And then he was gone. I do believe he has found a way to reach me through this song. Yes, my guardian angel lets me know that I do not walk alone.

Marcia Day, writer and producer
Nashville, Tennessee

Around that same time, one of my favorite singers, Julie London, scored her only charted hit, "Cry Me a River" (1955, no. 9). Her smoky, lingering voice told of a lover who took her for granted and then came back begging to be forgiven. But rather than being a complete compliant doormat, she does demand that he prove himself by crying a river for her, just as she cried a river over him. Something must have been in the air in 1955, for it seemed like the precursor to later vents of anger. Not only Julie London's song, but two more with a sense of strength hit the charts. The usually sweet McGuire Sisters hit number seventeen with their song about how they weren't gonna take it "No More."

You ain't gonna bother me no more
Nohow
Love just goes so far
No more
Woke up this morning and found
I didn't care for you no more
Nohow
Never felt so good before
You're down to my size
It's over and done
So honey, step down from your throne . . .

Whereas London's song wanted him to cry a river and the McGuire Sisters found a sense of freedom after dumping him because he was too dominating, another 1955 song was about raw power and female dominance. "Whatever Lola Wants" hit the charts twice: number six for Sarah Vaughan and number twelve for Dinah Shore.

Whatever Lola wants, Lola gets
And little man, little Lola wants you . . .
I always get, what I aim for
And your heart and soul, is what I came for . . .
Give in, give in, you'll never win

But let's not get too excited here about what looks like the beginnings of female independence. At first it might seem that "Cry Me a River" and "No More" might be prefeminist songs, breaking away from the tone of compliant and pathetic neediness. But they are filled with angry, vengeful sentiments, with little inner strength.

Now, Lola was another story. That song was from the Broadway show *Damn Yankees*, which ran for a very respectable 1,019 performances in the 1954–1955 season and was made into a movie in 1958. Gwen Verdon played Lola in both with relish and pizzazz. Unfortunately, the main theme was another of those archetypes of an ugly woman, Jezebel, wanting to be beautiful. In this case she sold her soul to the devil (a common theme in literature and movies) in order to be ravishing, which is presumably what women should be. Her only power was sexual (and it was ill-gotten to begin with) and she used it recklessly to try to bring down honorable baseball player Joe Hardy, who is sorely tempted. She was a real Jezebel. In the end, Joe sees the truth and leaves Lola to herself, who then reverts to a repulsive old hag.

It's not an attractive depiction of women, who are shown here as obsessed with physical beauty, and whose only other desires are to corrupt otherwise decent men. The men were not brought down by their own weakness but by the evil strength of Jezebel women. These archetypal characters keep reappearing. Women have been kept down so long that some men have a deep fear of women's strength. Somehow her strength will be like Delilah's and be the cause of his ruin. It is the old dichotomy of Compliant versus Jezebel.

Though Lola's sexual power was seen as negative, Marilyn Monroe's open sensuality captured the imagination of much of the world. In a way, she was the fifties version of Betty Boop, vulnerable and Compliant innocent, yet very, very sexy and provocative. The mature and worldly sexuality of Lola was to be despised, but the sexuality of Marilyn, who seemed too vulnerable to take her own power, was highly desirable. In two of her movies of 1953–1954—*Gentlemen Pre-*

fer Blondes and *How to Marry a Millionaire*—she is shown as a rather ditsy and naïve but extremely sensual ingenue. Though she did show a harder, more calculating side in *Niagara,* her legend remains as the vulnerable Compliant sexpot. Elizabeth Taylor was also often portrayed as a sexually oriented woman, but more of a Jezebel than Marilyn. In *Cat on a Hot Tin Roof* (1958) and her early sixties movies, *Butterfield 8, Cleopatra,* and *The Sandpiper,* her sexuality usually gets in the way or causes someone's downfall. In these roles she is a prostitute, a woman who has an affair with a married minister, and a manipulative queen who dominates both Caesar and Marc Antony, ultimately bringing ruin.

Raw sex was about to become acceptable in men, too. In those same years, a new phenomenon was starting that would have a great impact on popular music. Elvis Presley's hip gyrations that caused such a stir (who would even notice nowadays?) back in the mid-fifties and his deep earthy voice were male versions of the intense sensuality of Marilyn.

Even though times were changing, the final two years of the fifties brought a rash of silly songs, harking back to similar ones from 1951 to 1953. Remember, the country was still in the midst of McCarthyism and afraid of controversy. It was the year of the Hoola Hoop. Although it was only one year ago that the number of women voting in the United States finally equaled the number of male voters, females were singing inane songs—and people were buying a lot of records. One of my male friends thinks women gave a gift to everyone back then by reintroducing fun into music.

Betty Johnson had four Top 40 songs between 1956 and 1958, and one of her songs epitomized the inane songs that year.

"THE LITTLE BLUE MAN" (1958, no. 17)
One morning when I was out shopping
Though you'll find it hard to believe
A little blue man came out of the crowd

And timidly tugged at my sleeve
"I wuv you! I wuv you!" said the little blue man
"I wuv you! I wuv you to bits!"
"I wuv you!" He loved me said the little blue man
And scared me right out of my wits.

Weeks later, she gets so frustrated with his relentless pursuit that she pushes him off the side of a building, and he sings his love verses all the way down.

I whispered, "Thank goodness that's over!"
I smiled as I hurried outside
But there on the street stood the little blue man
Who said with a tear in his eye
"I don't wuv you anymore!"

As insipid as this song is, it seems so Freudian that one can hardly fail to notice. A man stalks her, she feels powerless until her anger builds and she tries to kill him. But he is more powerful than she, for he survives a deadly fall. And then he comes back to make her feel guilty. More silly songs in 1958 included ones such as the Chordettes' number-two "Lollipop," and the McGuire Sisters' number twenty-five "Ding Dong." After all, this was the same year that Sheb Wooley's "The Purple People Eater" became number one (and, strangely enough, when Nabokov's *Lolita* became a controversial international best-seller). Silliness continued into the next year with "Pink Shoelaces" (Dodie Stevens, no. 3) and "Kookie, Kookie (Lend Me Your Comb)," which was number four for Connie Stevens and Edward Byrnes. The Chordettes' first hit went number one and was also not very profound. "Mr. Sandman" gave 1954 the barbershop sound that would distinguish the group that had begun as a late 1940's folk group in Sheboygan, Wisconsin (my home state). They achieved nine Top 40 hits from 1954 to 1961.

But 1958 had its share of needy songs as well, in which women surrendered their power to men. Three of the most notable all happened to hit number seven that year. Kathy Linden (in "Billy") told of how she only talks, walks, and dines with Billy, because he really knows how to talk, walk, and dine. Evidently, she had none of these skills. The very *mature*-sounding Poni-Tails sang "Born Too Late," bemoaning her fate because she was too young for him. A song that remains to this day an enduring classic is Peggy Lee's "Fever," where he has power over her to turn her on. Yet, Peggy Lee does not sing it from neediness. Though the words might suggest so, she nonetheless lets us know that she has the situation under control. But, silly or simpering, neither tune sold many records, for women had only about one-tenth of the hits that year. Even the next year had its share of Compliant songs, including those by the popular group the Fleetwoods, with two women on vocals. "Come Softly to Me" begs for his love, his kisses, to be held through the night, while "Mr. Blue" laments life without him. Both are voices of women, lost without his love. Lana Bogan is an example of someone who suffered as a result of loving a man and ultimately being rejected by him. The Fleetwoods spoke to her pain.

ℛEMINISCENCE

"Come Softly to Me" and "Mr. Blue,"
the Fleetwoods, 1959, no. 1

You asked for it, Dorothy! And I haven't thought about this in a lifetime. I sit here knowing I don't have to sift through anything but one thing. I turned fourteen on July 14, 1959. The next month I lost my virginity. His name was Billy. He was seventeen and also a virgin. The standard line from the boy was "If you love me, you'll do it." So we "did it."

But please know that I don't ever remember feeling like a

little girl. Not ever. And I really, really loved Billy. When I lost what people have dubbed "my innocence," I remember feeling like a child for the first time in my life. A lost child, alone, abandoned, aching for someone (my mother) to find me.

"Come Softly to Me" and "Mr. Blue" by the Fleetwoods (both 1959, no. 1) were two songs that opened the floodgates and kept the little girl crying for a long time.

All of the songs that impacted me in my early life revolve around the pain associated with that abandonment. I remember playing the records (45 rpm) over and over so that I could cry harder, feel the pain deeper. Was it natural for me to make myself hurt more intensely? Did I feel guilty in my soul?

After we "did it" he seemed to have an instant aversion toward me. Aversion wasn't part of my active vocabulary. I didn't know there was a word for how he made me feel, other than to say it felt as though I made him sick to his stomach. We broke up. He wanted his ring back that I wore on a long chain around my neck. It was terribly humiliating. I suffered for over eighteen months. I wanted to die; truly die. And to this day I have never experienced that kind of pain and despair.

There was a public crucifixion for girls if they were known to "put out."

Losing your virginity even in a monogamous, boyfriend-girlfriend, going-steady relationship still meant "you put out."

For boys, it was mandatory to lose your virginity; they were supposed to "do it," expected to "do it,"—it was a rite of passage kind of thing. Something to celebrate. How wonderfully hypocritical. He was sexually baptized. And I was a "slut." I wonder now how many Billys there were. Was it natural for him to feel such repugnance? Did I make him feel guilty in his soul?

> *Lana Bogan,*
> *Director, Meharry Medical College,*
> *residential treatment program for*
> *pregnant crack addicts*

Amidst the pain many of us were experiencing, something wonderful happened in 1959. Despite the fact that Fidel Castro came to power that year and that the biggest fad on college campuses was jamming people into phone booths, there was a positive new trend. Of all the Top 40 hits by solo women artists, over one-third were sung by African-American women. This was a breakthrough year and it preceded the much more publicized Black Girl Groups that dominated the charts in the 1960s, as well as the ascendancy of Etta James, who some consider to be the greatest blues singer since Billie Holiday. All of these 1959 stars were accomplished vocalists, with a string of hits before and after. That year witnessed Sarah Vaughan ("Broken-Hearted Melody," no. 7), Miss Toni Fisher ("The Big Hurt," no. 3), Della Reese ("Don't You Know?" no. 2; "Not One Minute More," no. 16), Dinah Washington ("What a Difference a Day Makes," no. 8; "Unforgettable," no. 17), Lavern Baker ("I Cried a Tear," no. 6; "I Waited Too Long," no. 33), and Nina Simone ("I Loves You, Porgy," no. 18). Though this was her only Top 40 song in a forty-five year career, when people call out for "Porgy" at concerts, Simone has been known to reply, "I don't like cripples!"

Although everything was to blow apart in the sixties, the songs of the early sixties closely resembled those of the previous decades. What had changed was that now it was mostly teenagers who were singing the compliant songs. The 78 million baby boomers were growing up and a new phenomenon was occurring. This was the largest generation to date, one unscarred by the Depression, and they tended to be big spenders. When they bought records, they wanted to hear other teenagers sing. They weren't interested, as their mothers were, in listening to Patti Page or Dinah Shore. A multitude of young performers burst onto the scene. Initially, the young women continued to gasp for all-encompassing love. "I Want to Be Wanted" (Brenda Lee's number-one song in 1960) said it all for that era's compliant codependency. These young women had no sense of self outside a relationship, only a desperate neediness with a childlike demand for immediate gratification.

"I WANT TO BE WANTED"
Alone, so alone that I could cry
I want to be wanted . . .
Alone, just my lonely heart knows how
I want to be wanted—right now
Not tomorrow, but right now
I want to be wanted.

Some hits on the other side of the Atlantic were also needy, such as Cilla Black's "Step Inside Love" (U.K., 1968, no. 8), where she yearns for unconditional love, a song written by John Lennon and Paul McCartney for her weekly TV show. She became known as the "Dionne Warwick of England," where she had a series of hits, and her music had great impact on many people, such as New Zealand's Peter Jackson. Though "You're My World" had its lyrics, saying her world was over without his love, there were some lines about her reaching out, and with his hand in hers, she feels a power "so divine." It's not hard to see how a young boy who had recently lost a mother could find this song comforting.

ℛEMINISCENCE

"You're My World," Cilla Black, 1964, no. 26

My mother, Betty, committed suicide at age forty-seven in 1966, when I was fifteen. We lived in New Plymouth then. I had a premonition of Mum's distress when driving home, a hundred miles north, with Dad in the car. As the radio played the Beatles' "Eleanor Rigby" [1966, no. 11], I called out, "Dad, there's something wrong! It's Mum, we've got to get home!" I'm now fifty, and it's a strange feeling to have years she never had. She was brought up on a dairy farm in South Taranaki. Today I live on a ten-acre block with my wife and son and do some part-time farm work on a nearby spread. Each day as I milk the 730 cows, I think of Mum.

After the suicide, I was the only child of four siblings left living at home with my father. I had built my first valve radio set, which I had in my basement laboratory, together with a twelve-inch speaker, which I had mounted in an old basement shower cubicle in the same room. It was a space where I could spend time alone. I used to enjoy listening to the Friday evening English "hits."

A particular song that had impact in the next couple of years was Cilla Black's "You're My World." I no doubt felt the love and comfort of the song, and also the romance of a British singer. It gave me those warm fuzzies.

> *Peter Jackson, civil engineer*
> *and Maori development worker*
> MAUNGATUROTO, NORTHLAND
> NEW ZEALAND

Even as songs were being sung about compliancy, social forces were changing, and these would ultimately lead to greater strength in women. Career and family had been seen as mutually exclusive by middle-class women (working-class women were more likely to successfully combine work and motherhood), and sociologist Alfreda Iglehart later published a study that confirmed that married women of the fifties preferred to stay at home and not "inflict harm on their loved ones" by working. Despite these strong norms, women kept moving into the workplace. Prominent industrial psychologist Dr. Lillian Gilbreth (whose life as a working mother was chronicled in the 1950 movie *Cheaper by the Dozen* and 1952's *Belles on Their Toes*) wrote in 1952 that companies have the responsibility of eliminating discrimination against female employees, as well as providing benefits of maternity leave and part-time jobs, so that women can be productive workers and lead satisfying lives. With corporate assistance, family approval, and community support, wrote Gilbreth, women can prove to be "an asset and not a liability in every relationship of life." In 1954, the U.S. Women's Bureau realized that working women were a permanent part of the economy and started encouraging young girls to "Prepare for both job and marriage! Nowadays more and more married women continue with their jobs and return to work when their children are old enough." Three years later, in 1957, the launching of the Russian satellite *Sputnik* brought a more rigorous science and math curriculum for both boys and girls.

There were some women who were not letting the silly songs rule their lives. Four-months-pregnant Lillian Vernon was trying to think of an idea that would help pay household bills and allow her to continue working from home. She decided to start a mail-order business and used $2000 of her wedding-gift money as venture capital. Placing a $495 ad in *Seventeen* magazine for a personalized purse and belt, she filled the resulting $32,000 in orders at the kitchen table in her Mount Vernon, New York, apartment. Her business, Lillian Vernon, was launched and now has sales of $240 million.

Another homemaker found her own power ten years later. Jean Nidetch lost seventy-two pounds by eating healthily and then in 1961 started working on her friends, fat housewives who gathered in her apartment in Queens, New York. Within two years, the self-described "formerly fat housewife" founded Weight Watchers International and revolutionized dieting. Instead of starving or counting calories, Nidetch preached the need to change eating habits and to seek out encouragement from friends. It was one of the first support groups.

By the end of the fifties the larger economy became more welcoming. Demand for clerical, teaching, and nursing jobs mushroomed and the economic apartheid demanded that women fill these lower-paying positions. As we shall see, by the sixties women started to notice in large numbers that they were not getting a fair deal.

Most of the Top 40 female songs in 1960 were codependent and gushy, such as "Many Tears Ago" (Connie Francis, no. 8), "Everybody's Somebody's Fool" (Connie Francis, no. 1), and "In My Little Corner of the World" (Anita Bryant, no. 10). But "Don't Break the Heart That Loves You" (Connie Francis, no. 1), because the result will be "All Alone Am I" (Brenda Lee, no. 3), since I know "You Don't Love Me No More" (Barbara George, no. 3). In the end, I'll take the blame for anything, just to get you back; yes, I'll keep saying "I'm Sorry" (Brenda Lee, no. 1). And there are "Sixteen Reasons" (Connie Stevens, no. 3) why "Johnny Loves Me" (Shelley Fabares, no. 21). The Chantels had a string of Top 40 hits, most of them codependent but with some self-esteem, such as 1961's "Look in My Eyes" (no. 14), saying that if you don't love me, I'll leave.

One of the rarer, more adult songs looked at the consequences of lacking good love boundaries. Sung by one of the first Girl Groups, its theme was less immature than the more common needy song of those years. Originally known as the Poquellos (birds), they were on the verge of stardom in 1958 when they changed to their final, more marketable name of The Shirelles, after one member, Shirley Owens. After a couple of smaller hits ("I Met Him on a Sunday" and "Dedicated to the One I Love"), their 1960 "Tonight's the Night" (no. 39) was reissued the following year as "Will You Love Me Tomorrow?"

and went to number one for nineteen weeks, making this the first Girl Group to top the *Billboard* Top 100. The song wondered whether he would still love her tomorrow if she were to give herself to him completely. I remember our minister, Pastor Andersen, bemoaning back in 1961 what the world had come to that such wanton songs were allowed on the radio waves. It all seems so quaint now, when I compare these songs with some of the explicit lyrics of more modern songs. Back then, though, that song was a watershed of sorts. It caused people to start questioning the unbridled giving that characterized Compliance, even though this message was initially overpowered by all the gush.

Similar themes abounded in the next two years. Once again, in both years, most female songs were mushy and even desperately Compliant. Of course, those of us listening to the songs back then didn't see the desperation in our own feelings. My next-door neighbor, Sandy Hardiman, and I would put 45 rpm records on her player, take off our shoes, and dance the hours away in her upstairs linoleum-tiled bedroom to such themes as: my "Tall Paul" (Annette Funicello, 1959, no. 7) said "Oh! Carol" (Neil Sedaka, 1959, no. 9) and asked me to "Put Your Head on My Shoulder" (Paul Anka, 1959, no. 2), so I asked myself "If I Give My Heart to You" (Kitty Kallen, 1959, no. 34), will you be careful? Or will I be saying "I Cried a Tear" (Lavern Baker, 1959, no. 6), "Many Tears Ago" (Connie Francis, 1960, no. 7) because "Everybody's Somebody's Fool" (Connie Francis, 1960, no. 1)— even if he does wear "Pink Shoelaces" (Dodie Stevens, no. 3). I was not conscious of the way these songs were affecting my self-esteem as a woman. Even a few years later, in 1964, when I would sit in the Waukesha High School lunchroom every day with my good friend Linda Thompkins, we would talk about boys and who we liked. Stand up for ourselves? Be our own person? Are you kidding? Our highest goals weren't that different from Marcie Blane's in "Bobby's Girl" (1962, no. 3):

When people ask of me,
What would you like to be
Now that you're not a kid anymore.
I know just what to say,
I answer right away,
There's just one thing I've been wishing for.
I want to be Bobby's girl
I want to be Bobby's girl,
That's the most important thing to me.

We were also listening to "My Boy Lollipop" (Millie Small, no. 2), "Wishin' and Hopin' " (Dusty Springfield, no. 6) that we would find a boy to figure out if "it's in his kiss" ("Shoop Shoop Song," no. 6), and often we were wailing about someone or other, wondering "Where Did Our Love Go?" (the Supremes, no. 1). Back then, neither Linda, I, nor anyone around us were aware of the chains that bound us nor how, in just a few years, we would try to break them.

Many of us were trying to find our true love. There is nothing wrong with that. It was just that many of the messages told us that we had to give up ourselves in order to do that.

A Broadway show that was later made into a movie offered a similar message. The syrupy but entertaining *The Sound of Music* came out in 1965 and etched in our brains a number of songs many of us still hum to this day. Think of "My Favorite Things"; "I Am Sixteen (Going on Seventeen)"; "Edelweiss"; "So Long, Farewell"; and the memorable "Climb Every Mountain," which lives on to this day at graduations, birthday parties, and other events. Even though it did not make the Top 40, the fact that it has lasted this long attests to its power. Sung in the movie by a nun, it is a message of strength and hope, something long needed in the woman's voice. The ultimate message of the movie, though, was one of a woman serving a man and thus having all her needs filled. The Compliant is happiest as server. Gina Mendello listened to these songs and paid for it with a great deal of pain and heartache.

ℛEMINISCENCE

The Sound of Music, 1965

In 1960s Hollywood, the measure of how good your life was came from how close it was to the movies. And so there I was born in drama and raised in drama. Actually, looking back now it's somewhat comic. My parents were characters that could have been played by Joan Crawford and Burt Lancaster in a script written by Neil Simon and directed by Alfred Hitchcock. Everything was about being larger than life, or glamorous, or tragic.

My idea of perfect love came from *The Sound of Music*. The scene in the gazebo in which Baron Von Trapp finally proclaims his love to Maria still is the most romantic moment in film for me. There was sexual tension and conflict and miscommunication up until this point. They fought and nearly lost each other, and then they released their feelings and expected eternal bliss. They sang "Something Good," about standing there loving the other, whether or not they should. Somewhere in their youth, they must have been good. Well there's motivation for a little girl: Be good and act like a nun and you'll get yourself a baron one day.

But soon reality set in and I learned that relationships that are created out of tension and conflict also end that way. Everything seemed to fall short of the movies. The knight on the white horse never came to sweep me off into the desert. But there was plenty of drama, that's for sure. And not in a good way. When I was in college I fell for a man who was sexually confused. I believed and he believed that if I loved him enough, he could change. In an idealized Hollywood ending he pulls me to him just as I'm about to walk away and we live happily ever after. I prayed, I sacrificed, I suffered, I believed in him, but I got no miracle ending.

It was very un-Hollywood to meet a nice compatible partner, get married, and have a happy life. Unless, that is, aliens then landed in your backyard, or the devil takes possession of your little girl by sucking her into the television. Trying to live on a movie set just didn't work for me. I'm afraid that my denial of the ordinary in pursuit of the extraordinary left me cynical and alone.

Gina Mendello, artists' manager
NASHVILLE, TENNESSEE

It took Mendello years to figure out the emptiness of the Compliant's quest for true love. Not all songs were so fairy tale. Some of the songs about finding a soul mate had a sweetness about them, such as Shelby Flint's, which nonetheless was still asking luck or fate to bring her love.

ℛEMINISCENCE

"Angel on My Shoulder," Shelby Flint, 1961, no. 22

The song "Angel on My Shoulder" expressed my wish and desire to find a mate to love and be loved by. The song was often played during the early 1970s, a time when I was a young single mother in graduate school and had a four-year-old daughter. As I began to explore my inner self, I discovered that I longed for an intimate relationship beyond friendship. Although loving my daughter as well as friends and family and those around me was satisfying, I longed to be known fully by another human being in a complete and intimate way. I felt that if God gave me the opportunity to meet a "true love," I would take the risk of loving again.

The song expresses the feeling that meeting such a person is a matter of fortune, luck, wishing, and praying and is mostly out of your own control. This is a difficult fact for people to grasp and I have found it to be almost universal. Later, when I was a married woman, friends would ask how we met. Meeting Hugh was, as the song indicates, completely out of my own control. I had accepted that I may never have a mate and was truly happy in my single state with a full life with my daughter, my work, and my friends and my family. When I met Hugh at a faith-based international meeting, I was quite surprised at his immediate response. While I recognized that this man could be my mate, I was more cautious and prayed, "Could you really want this for me?" Roses and long handwritten letters from London and ardent declarations from Hugh convinced me that this indeed was my mate. We were married in London and are now celebrating our tenth anniversary in 2002.

When my singing group in London heard this song, they asked me to teach it to them. The message of the song was felt by the group, most of whom were single and longed to find their mates. I passed the song on to them. One of them wrote me later to tell me that he had met his true love. They were at a religious summer school and when he went to pray late at night, she was there. They were immediately drawn to each other spiritually and married the following year.

Lynda Adamson
Savannah, Georgia

We might have had the *cold* war back then, but other things were *hot*. Helen Gurley Brown's book *Sex and the Single Girl* was the biggest selling book in 1962, the same year thirty-six-year-old Marilyn Monroe's heat was put out when she died of an apparent drug overdose.

In 1961 Patsy Cline finally showed the whole country what Nashville had known for some years, namely, that she was one great singer. Patsy was one of the early crossover stars from country to pop and had just the correct amount of ripe codependency in her songs. Between 1961 and 1962 she had three top hits ("Crazy," no. 9, "I Fall to Pieces," no. 12, "She's Got You," no. 14), but then she died in a tragic plane crash in 1963. All three songs had the same basic theme: I love you so bad I go insane, I fall apart, but since I can't have you, I go even more crazy.

The contest for the neediest songs from 1960 through 1963 goes to two singers: Connie Francis, who became the number-two singer (overall, not just in the female category) in 1960, and Brenda Lee, who won the same award in 1961. Their songs said, unless I am wanted, I am nothing; I am completely alone since you left me; you flirt and take my love for granted, but I don't know how I could live if you said good-bye; I was a fool to think you loved me too; I want to be someone other than myself; I'm busy breaking in my brand-new broken heart; you have another love and you even call me by her name, but I'd rather have this love than none at all; my whole world is falling apart because I am losing you and I need you bad; I must be the biggest fool of all; nobody can hurt me the way you do; I'll be following the boys, no matter where they go; even though you dumped me and found someone new, you can depend on me and I'll always be yours. Think about it: how could any of us have hoped for a sense of inner strength when these were the messages drilled into our teenage brains every day?

The next couple of years weren't much better even though female musicians sold more records. Though 1963 witnessed the official birth of the women's movement with the publication of Betty Friedan's *The Feminine Mystique*, but you could hardly tell it from the message in the songs. Skeeter Davis's number two "End of the World," chronicled how meaningless her life was after he goes, which was very similar to Brenda Lee's "My Whole World Is Falling Down" (because he is gone).

"END OF THE WORLD"
Why does the sun go on shining
Why does the sea rush to shore
Don't they know it's the end of the world
'Cause you don't love me any more

Skeeter Davis's number-seven "I Can't Stay Mad at You" was about a guy who lied and ran around, but she was going to love him no matter what; "Your Old Stand By" (Mary Wells) told of how the man she loved would use her when he was down or his girlfriend was mean to him; the Crystals let everybody know "He's Sure the Boy I Love" (1963, no. 11), who holds her tight, but all he has is an unemployment check; the Angels announced "I Adore Him" (1963, no. 25), even though he cheated on her.

This theme of knowing he is a creep and not caring extended to Dee Dee Sharp (in "Wild!"), allowing herself to fall in love with someone she knew would dump her. And, one of my favorites that perfectly captures the era: Little Peggy March's number one "I Will Follow Him," explained how she would go wherever he does, for he is her destiny. Interestingly, that song was first sung in French (with the title "Chariot") by the British Petula Clark, who had a string of Top 40 hits later in the sixties. Then there was Nancy Sinatra, daughter of Old Blue Eyes, who sang the winner of the low self-esteem award song: "Friday's Child" (1966, no. 36). Friday's child was born ugly with bad luck and is so worthless that they will forget to bury her when she dies. She hadn't yet found those boots with which she was gonna walk all over him.

There were a few songs that year, however, that hinted at some anger, some getting back, but it was pretty mild. Etta James's "Pushover" was about a woman who told him that even though the other girls thought he was fine, she knew he was untrue and she was not about to be what he expected: a pushover. Making him feel sorry was the theme in "One Fine Day," sung by the Chiffons (written by Carole King), who said that eventually he would want her and realize how great she was. The same theme is also evident in "My Boyfriend's Back," where the Angels are really gonna put it to him. Okay, the *boyfriend* is going to let him have it, while I stand back and watch. Still, there is a great deal of pent-up anger in that song. It was too risky to lash out at one's own boyfriend, but you could let you boyfriend lash out.

One song that is hard to analyze is Barbra Streisand's 1964 number-five hit, "People." On the one hand, it seems to have a message of Compliant codependency, of needing others in order to be whole. On the other hand, it suggests that we ought to be mature adults, not children with silly and divisive pride issues. This song, like so many others, allows us to project our own inner needs. Because Streisand sings it with such emotion, it also allows the listener's emotions to come closer to the surface.

ℛEMINISCENCE

"People," Barbra Streisand, 1964, no. 5

All my life, I've been a loner torn between wanting to be alone—feeling satisfied and whole in solitude—and wanting to share the satisfaction of connecting with others, feeling the pain of otherness and self-imposed isolation. One day, in my teens, I heard Barbra Streisand's golden voice croon, "People who need people are the luckiest people in the world." Luckiest, yes! The song struck me to the heart, so perfectly did it express the part of me that yearned to be someone I was not. It became my private theme song, a mantra to hold back the pain. When I felt isolated, I called up the memory of that song and played it from beginning to end. Somehow it soothed me, perhaps because it bridged the confusion and ambiguity, bringing me face-to-face with the reality that I would never be "a person who needs people." I share with Emerson the ideal of self-reliance, of finding strength within myself. Have I really any choice? I don't think of my theme song often anymore . . .just occasionally. I still haven't told anyone about it.

> *Ruth Axelrod, faculty member,*
> *George Washington University,*
> WASHINGTON, D.C.

Even as the women's movement was picking up speed through the late sixties, there were still so many desperately compliant songs that it makes me nauseous to read through all of them. Why does it make me sick? Because it brings back painful memories of just how desperate I was in those days.

Compliant songs in the rest of the decade can be divided into two types. First: You must love me or I can't go on, which was a continuation of that same theme that went throughout the whole century. But a new one emerged, one that had only been hinted at before in the Top 40: He's a creep, but I'll love him forever. These ideas had been around for decades in the blues, owing their themes to blues pioneers such as Bessie Smith, whose 1923 number-one "Down-Hearted Blues" moaned about the low-life man she had the bad sense to trust. Ma Rainey's 1925 number-fourteen, "See See Rider Blues," tells of a two-timing man she has let herself love.

A major difference between make-me-your-victim songs and the real blues was that the (usually) African-American woman acknowledges her lower status, but does it in a way that maintains her own dignity and sets important boundaries. The first category includes needy songs that beg for domination and the plea to "Rescue Me" (Fontella Bass, 1965, no. 4). Barbara Lewis sang "Make Me Belong to You" (1966, no. 28), because my life is endless without your love. Aretha Franklin came out with "My Song," (1969, no. 31)—in order to have you, I need to be who *you* want me to be; whereas Dusty Springfield wrote about "Wishin' and Hopin'" (1964, no. 6). The Supremes delivered "My World Is Empty Without You" in 1966 (no. 5), while Martha and the Vandellas sang about being pulled into the "Quicksand" (1964, no.8) because of your charms.

"WISHIN' AND HOPIN'"
[You gotta]
Show him that you care just for him
Do the things he likes to do
Wear your hair just for him, 'cause
You won't get him
Thinkin' and a-prayin'
Wishin' and a-hopin'

The late 1960s also brought forth more "he is a creep" songs. The classic song by Tammy Wynette advised women that if they wanted their man, though he's weak and doing bad things, they must "Stand by Your Man" (1968, no. 19). This song was Tammy's, First Lady of Country Music, most popular crossover hit, cowritten with my neighbor Billy Sherrill. Women realized it was their job to accept men, no matter what.

Another famous song is Janis Joplin's (with Big Brother and the Holding Company) plea to her abusive man to take another "Piece of My Heart" (1968, no. 12) if it makes him feel good. With its raw emotion, the song became a means for creating female bonding between two female students at Oberlin College. The therapeutic process of naming the pain, as the blues had done, helped these women feel stronger.

REMINISCENCE

"Piece of My Heart," Janis Joplin, 1968, no. 12

It was 1968, and the start of my first year at Oberlin. I knew no one at the college, and I was a little scared as I left New Jersey and headed west. Joanie had left Kansas City and headed east. There we were together in a dorm room. We had each brought some records from home. We had different musical tastes, but we both had Janis Joplin's *Cheap Thrills*. We did have something in common. Janis and "Piece of My Heart" helped us both. We played it *all the time*, over and over. Singing very loudly, feeling strong, and becoming friends. Ruthie, in the room next to ours, soon had enough. One afternoon, she climbed in through the window and took the record. She left a note that said something like, "Ha, ha. I took the record!!!" She didn't know we had another copy.

When we came back from dinner and found the note, Joanie and I cranked up the stereo louder than ever, with Janis and the two of us belting out "Piece of My Heart." Ruthie, sensing she'd lost the battle, came next door and started singing, too. The song made us feel strong and that we could do anything.

Friendships blossomed, and we had a terrific freshman year.

That early bonding experience—loud and powerful—has remained a "piece of our hearts." Many times over the course of our friendship, Ruthie and I have talked about freshman year and laughed about her stealing the record.

To this day, the song makes us think about strength, power, and passion. A couple of years ago, Ruthie found a

1969 photo of Janis for sale, and she sent it to me. It hangs in my office at work.

Diana Stork, professor,
Simmons Graduate School of
Management,
BOSTON, MASSACHUSETTS

There were lots more songs listing all the faults of men but promising to love him anyway. Leslie Gore, who also sang about independence, had several Compliant songs as well. "Maybe I Know" (1964, no. 14) that he lies and cheats, and that he has an eye for girls, but, heck, "That's the Way Boys Are" (1964, no. 12) and, anyway, I know deep down he loves me. The Supremes need him so much they are willing to put up with "Nothing but Heartaches" (1965, no. 11).

In other songs, men were held to different standards. They were expected to be jerks, but women were supposed to love them anyway. Whether it was Mama or their friends, these women knew what they were getting into and went anyway with the "Leader of the Pack" (the Shangri-Las, 1964, no. 1) and "Wild One" (Martha and the Vandellas, 1964, no. 34), wailing "Oh No Not My Baby" (Maxine Brown, 1965, no. 24). The Shangri-Las, in fact, often sang about the darker side of teenage girlhood ("I Can Never Go Home Anymore" and "Give Us Your Blessings") and all the bad things that happen to you if you are more the "tough" type, which is how they dressed, too.

Skip forward a couple of decades to Cyndi Lauper's "Girls Just Want to Have Fun," a statement of equality of activities. But the sixties had not gotten that far yet. Betty Wright's 1968 number thirty-three hit let us all know that if we wanted to be ladies, well: "Girls Can't Do What the Guys Do."

A desperate but haunting song came out in 1967 and climbed high on the charts to number three. It is a song about waiting by the

phone for him to call, something young women did before call waiting or answering machines were available. Maybe they wouldn't even
walk outside to get the mail. And they'd make anyone besides *him*
hang up who tried to call the house. Vikki Carr—who is still popular
today, especially in Latin America (one reason is the depth of her
emotion as she sings)—articulated this experience. In the song, she
laments losing him, telling herself it doesn't matter, there are lots of
guys out there. But then the phone rings and she is startled, running
to the receiver, grabbing it and praying to God from the desperate
depths of her heart that it would be *HIM,* or else she is just going to
die. When it isn't him, she says she *will* die. But then she gets herself
together and decides she can live without him—that is, until the
phone rings and she goes through it all again.

When I sing that song as part of my performance, most women
respond that they, too, have sat hoping anxiously by the phone, just
waiting and waiting for him to call. Nowadays young women seem to
have moved ahead a little. The teenage women in my groups say they
only do that sometimes. "Is any guy worth that?" I ask them and they
answer "no." Then I turn to the teenage guys and ask them the same
question. "Is any guy worth a female acting like Vikki Carr does in the
song?" It is heartening to hear them respond with the same "no!"

"It Must Be Him" was one of the songs on the CD I recently
recorded. As we recorded it, Gary Earl, one of the producers, said,
"That song is dreadfully pathetic." Yes, I told him, that is the whole
point. Carr had two other hits, one of which perfectly suited her
needy and even victim demeanor. "With Pen in Hand" (1969, no. 35)
is a melodramatic story of a woman whose husband leaves her; as she
signs the divorce papers, she tells him that if he doesn't think he can
love her anymore, and if he thinks he can take care of their daughter,
then she'll be gone and on her way. The way Carr sings, with such
deep emotion, is quite impressive. She wants him to forgive her, but
he doesn't, for men aren't expected to. What women must do is dif-

ferent—her other hit was about how the woman must forgive her man ("The Lesson," 1968, no. 34).

Arguably the most pathetic song during those years was by Sandy Posey, who is not well-known today but had four Top 40 hits between 1966 and 1967. The one that hit number twelve in 1966, meaning it was "hot," made my teenage daughter, Solange (eighteen), cringe recently. I had to convince her that it was not a parody, that we really believed those ideas back then. When I played it for Elizabeth, age sixteen, she kept saying, "What a loser." It was hard for her to grasp how "normal" this message was back in the sixties. My oldest daughter, Roxanne (twenty-one), was shocked when she heard the lyrics. "I can't believe that was a hit. I take it for granted that I have the same opportunities as men. If that song came out now, it would go nowhere."

"Born a Woman"
It doesn't matter if you're rich or poor
Or if you're smart or dumb
A woman's place in this old world
Is under some man's thumb

And if you're born a woman
You're born to be hurt
You're born to be stepped on, lied to, cheated on
And treated like dirt

Ah if you're born a woman
You're born to be hurt . . .
Well I was born a woman
I didn't have no say

Imagine singing, seriously, that women were born to be cheated on and treated like dirt. The line "I didn't have no say" describes the powerlessness she felt. Regenia Grissom saw that same powerlessness in her mother-in-law, whose husband kept her in her place.

ℛEMINISCENCE

"Born a Woman," Sandy Posey, 1966, no. 12;
and "Diamonds Are a Girl's Best Friend,"
Marilyn Monroe, 1953

Sandy Posey sang that a woman's place is under some man's thumb and I learned about this from my in-laws. When I was single, I moved to a nearby town to be closer to my workplace—State Farm Insurance. Not only did I buy my own house, but I also convinced my mother to move to the same town. Coincidentally, she moved across the street from a family that was later to become my in-laws.

My future father-in-law was a thirty-plus-year retired Air Force veteran. As he traveled around the world in the military, his wife stayed in the States and raised their three sons. She took care of all the business while he was gone, but the minute he got home it was like she was pushed behind the door until he would leave for his next tour of duty. He thought the wife's place was in the home and never allowed her to get a job outside the house.

My husband lived at home with his parents until we got married. From overhearing some of my husband and father-in-law's conversations about finances, I knew there were going to be problems. He advised my husband that he was "head" over the wife and that he should take charge of all the finances, even though I was doing very well taking care of myself and had, in fact, bought my own house—while he was still living at home and spending his money on race cars. He had never had any financial responsibility. Needless to say, money caused lots of problems for us and almost led to divorce. However, we celebrated our twenty-fifth wedding anniversary in 2000.

My father-in-law retired from the military about the same time we got married. My mother-in-law was so depressed over not getting a new house after he retired that she let it destroy her life. He wanted a farm, but she wanted a house and a lot in an upscale neighborhood. They never could agree so they stayed where they were. Ultimately, she was overcome by complications and side effects from diabetes, which led to her death in 1990.

All their material comforts finally did not help her. As the song said, "diamonds are a girl's best friend," and he did pay for diamonds for my mother-in-law (he never went and picked them to surprise her). But, diamonds don't remove depression and heartaches. Because we were close, I (and my daughter) inherited some of her diamonds, and I constantly remember her pain.

Yes, my father-in-law thought a woman's place was under some man's thumb. And his wife never got out from under it. It still makes me sad when I think about it, because he wasn't a bad person. He just didn't know any better.

Regenia Grissom, CPCU,
State Farm Insurance
MURFREESBORO, TENNESSEE

Sandy Posey's mega-Compliant song, "Born a Woman" was nominated for two Grammys: Best Vocal and Best Contemporary Solo Vocal, and it went on to be recorded by six more female artists. Not coincidentally, 1966 was the year that the man as alley-cat movie, *Tom Jones,* won Oscars in four of the six major categories. The next year, Michael Caine won an Academy Award as the misogynist hero Alfie, who dumps on one woman after another, and about whom the movie's famous title song crooned ("Alfie," Dionne Warwick, 1967, no. 15). In other words, the exploited women's theme goes along with the theme of the male creep.

Posey's words are so hard to imagine that sometimes I have people come up to me after my performances and tell me that Sandy Posey could not have been serious. One man recently argued that Sandy Posey's song was more sarcastic. At first, I thought he had a point, but after extensive research on Posey's songs and her life, that idea just didn't stand up. Her short career in the sixties included five Top 40 hits, all of them the I-love-being-a-victim type, a theme that did not carry well into the seventies. Besides "Born a Woman," she sang about a "Single Girl" (1966, no. 12, cowritten with Martha Sharp) who needs a man to lean on; when she does show the slightest assertion, it relates to either her failed attempt to break up, backtracking after he cries in "I Take It Back" (1967, no. 12), or what she does with a lying, cheating, lazy man. Does she kick him out or demand he change? No, instead, her assertiveness takes the form of having her own affair as she explains in "What a Woman in Love Won't Do" (1967, no. 31). If you are one of those who think Sandy Posey was more subtle, singing in irony rather than self-pity, consider her other songs: "I Will Never Marry" because men only hurt you; and "I'm Just Here to Get My Baby Out of Jail."

Listening to Posey's song "Born a Woman" brought many memories back to me. How was it I could be that unconscious back then? That I didn't stand up and yell whenever that type of song came on? We were influenced by the culture around us and didn't see all the injustices.

The change in consciousness started in the mid-1960s, as women stopped wearing those restrictive girdles (the modern version of a corset). We began to throw off some of the Compliant strictures of an unfair society. There was a new and growing consciousness, an awareness, that all was not right. When Little Peggy March's "I Wish I Were a Princess" hit the charts in 1963, it was the last time a female had a hit with the word "princess" in the title. Gene Pitney's "Princess in Rags" (1965, no. 37) was the only other hit using "princess" for the rest of the century. Pitney sang about a poor princess whom he would someday rescue. It was the same theme as Peggy March's of a power-less woman who needs to be saved by a powerful and loving man.

It was the close of an era when March sang about wishing hard for power. Not feeling she had any influence of her own, she had to imagine being a princess in order to exert any control. What would she do with this newfound authority? Would she end world hunger or help downtrodden women? No, she would make him love and then marry her.

Looking back on these sentiments, the modern woman might ask why she wasn't angry at feeling powerless. But even though my daughters might now see Sandy Posey as a loser, those of us who grew up in those times, didn't know the power that might have been ours. One of my favorite fantasies as a child was the same as Little Peggy March's—that of being a princess and having a handsome prince love me. Compare that to my own daughters' fantasies of being a doctor, chef, bakery owner, or architect. It took a while for women's voice in popular music to change from wanting to be a princess to being angry that the princess was the only apparent route to power. Thus began the change in consciousness.

THIRD MOVEMENT
Johnny, I'll Get Angry

VERSE FIVE
1960s

"You Don't Own Me"

ARCHETYPES PRESENT:
Social/Rebel

*a*s to be expected, the music themes of the 1960s were about rebellion, independence, social reform, revenge, and the demand for respect. The women's movement was beginning to take form and the rebel archetype dominated. Still there was backlash from the conservatives who sang about tomorrow being bright; how they love the creep and they were caught in the chains of love. One song that captured the change in consciousness in the sixties was "You Don't Own Me" by Leslie Gore (1964, no. 2). Even when a man treats her like dirt, Gore takes a rebellious stand for freedom, for long-deserved independence. She asks him just to let her be herself, not tell her what to say or do and not try to change her in any way.

"YOU DON'T OWN ME"
You don't own me, don't try to change me in any way
You don't own me, don't tie me down 'cause I'd never stay

Oh, I don't tell you what to say
I don't tell you what to do
So just let me be myself
That's all I ask of you

The enduring nature of the song is evidenced by its use in movies such as 1996's *The First Wives Club,* where it is sung at the end to show how Diane Keaton, Bette Midler, and Goldie Hawn are their own persons, not beholden to men anymore. It was with the same spirit that at that same time my mother finally threw out my wife-beating and compulsive-gambler father after eighteen miserable years of marriage. She was fed up with being used both physically and emotionally as his punching bag.

Gore's popularity in this decade, with her bold and sassy songs ("It's My Party" and "It's Judy's Turn to Cry," among others), shows the development of women's independence. Right before her rise, the songs selling the most were the woe-is-me variety from Connie Francis and Brenda Lee. Leslie Gore was a sign of the new era.

Two years earlier than "You Don't Own Me" was Dionne Warwick's "Don't Make Me Over" (1962), which on first glance sounds like the same theme. But read on. But, whereas Gore *told* him to lay off, Warwick is compliantly "begging" him to not pick on her faults, because she adores him so. Accept me as I am, she pleads, because she is at his command. It was a first attempt at speaking up and being assertive, but was weak when compared to Gore's demonstrative attempt. On the other hand, Warwick's "Don't Make Me Over" was a move toward assertiveness when compared with 1962's number-seven "Johnny Get Angry," where Joanie Sommers compliantly shouts she wants a caveman who will show how much he really cares for her, well, then "Don't Make Me Over" is a move toward assertiveness.

There was something about Gore's song that marks a watershed in women's music and makes 1964 an important year. Something about her message touched the Rebel archetype. How many people remember Sandy Posey's "Born a Woman" (1966, no. 12)? It may have touched the pathetic Compliant archetype back then, but it was not sustained into successive decades. "You Don't Own Me" stuck around, and it mirrored social changes that were transforming society.

The tension between the fantasy ideal of womanhood in the fifties compared to the boring grind of their everyday life (as argued in 1995 in "Where the Girls Are") was one reason for the changing view of womanhood. Furthermore, the introduction of the pill in the 1960s offered women previously unknown sexual freedom. Betty Friedan's book *The Feminine Mystique* became a best-seller and challenged the accepted role of women in families and society. It was followed in coming years by Kate Millett's *Sexual Politics* (1970) and Germaine Greer's *The Female Eunuch.* As the women's movement gained momentum, changes took place.

Harvard Business School started admitting women in 1963 as MBA students. The 1964 Title VII of the Civil Rights Act made workplace discrimination on the basis of race, age, national origin, religion, or gender illegal. The last characteristic was included by a Virginia congressman who had hoped to stall the bill by identifying it with the unpopular 1960's women's movement (see J. Edward Pawlick's book *Freedom Will Conquer Racism (And Sexism)* for more detail on the attempted derailment of the Civil Rights bill.) But the Congressman's strategy backfired, however and "gender" became a vital part of the Civil Rights bill. It was not until 1980, however, that the EEOC issued new guidelines pronouncing sexual harassment illegal under Title VII. Even minority women gained prominence in Congress. In 1968, Shirley Chisholm (D-NY) became the first black woman elected to the U.S. Congress, and four years later Barbara Jordan (D-TX) became the first black woman elected from a southern state.

• • •

An enormous change for women took place in the work arena as a result of baby boomers looking for jobs. Women were flooding the workplace in the sixties, going from 21 million to 29 million. Employment for women grew at a rate of 37 percent, while it grew for men at only 9 percent. But old stereotypes die hard. Working mothers in the sixties felt guilty not being home with their children full-time, and even younger baby boomers grew up with the fifties assumptions that working was for single women and married women without children. New values did impact them, though. This group of early baby-boomer women who reached eighteen in the 1960s married older and had less children than women ten years older. It was the beginning of the "baby bust," when the birth rate declined for some years. Of course, it was blamed on the so-called unfeminine practice of working outside the home.

As the economy grew, demand for clerical and service jobs exploded, causing an occupational "pink ghetto" of lower-level clerical jobs distinguished from higher-paying service jobs. With all these women entering the workforce, it became obvious that women were not earning the same as men. A full-time employed woman was earning sixty cents to the man's dollar. Seeing the injustice, women got angry. Lobbying by women's groups produced the Equal Pay Act in 1963, designed to bring more equality. But such change does not usually come overnight. By 1970, women's earnings had actually dropped to 59 percent of what men were earning.

One woman who noticed the discrepancies between men and women was Felice N. Schwartz, who, in 1962, founded the New York-based research organization Catalyst in order to provide women with better access not only to the workplace, but also to top jobs. She argued later to make parenting interchangeable between women and men, citing statistics that 97 percent of male corporate leaders have families, while only 40 percent of women managers do. Women carry the burden of homemaking and child rearing, she noted, which limits their career potential.

In 1967 affirmative action was applied to women, opening more doors for women in untraditional work settings. One woman told me years ago in one of my seminars: "Men tell me it is unfair that I got my job because of affirmative action. But, let me explain. Previously, I was a secretary earning twenty thousand dollars. Now I'm a highway inspector and earn forty thousand dollars, and I get excellent performance evaluations. It's a job that no woman had before affirmative action. I'm a single mother with two kids. Am I supposed to feel bad I got this job?"

Some women hit it big as entrepreneurs, too. In 1963, saleswoman Mary Kay Ash took five thousand dollars of her own money to start a company that would make a difference in the lives of other women. Her motto became, "My objective in life is to help women know how great they really are." Through direct sales, she set up an organization based on the golden rule that focused on meeting the needs of the female sales force, that helped them increase their self-esteem. Part of the rewards program became the well-known pink Cadillacs. Her business formula was so effective that Mary Kay Cosmetics landed on the "100 Best Companies to Work for" list and became a multibillion-dollar venture.

Joan Ganz Cooney started an enterprise that was to revolutionize children's television and greatly impact early childhood education. Her TV show *Sesame Street* premiered in 1969 and is still watched by millions of children around the world.

In tiny all-white Riceville, Iowa, a petite, five-foot-two, blue-eyed fourth-grade teacher named Jane Elliott tried an experiment to help answer her students' questions about why Martin Luther King Jr. had recently been assassinated. Dividing the students into groups by eye color, she told them those with brown eyes were better than those with blue, finding that the "superior" children quickly fell into the role of oppressor. Her experiment had such impact that she continued it until she retired from teaching sixteen years later, and the experiment was chronicled in the documentary *Eye of the Storm*. In the process, she helped change the way people thought about prejudice and racism.

In other countries, too, women were breaking boundaries and rules. In 1966, Indira Gandhi, whose political pedigree was as the daughter of India's first president Jawaharlal Nehru, became the first woman prime minister of India, as well as the first woman in the world to be elected as head of state of a major country. Three years later, American-born (in Milwaukee, near my hometown) Golda Meir was rewarded for her leadership ability and years of service by being elected the first woman prime minister of Israel.

Whatever forces were at work, a new voice started to emerge in Top 40 songs in the sixties. I-love-you-even-if-you-are-a creep messages were starting to be replaced by a sense of injustice and even anger. The Rebel had arrived with strength. But social change takes time. Changes in women's consciousness happened over some decades, taking into account "backlash"—the energy exerted in order to maintain the status quo. Ultimately, such efforts are fruitless, for as Victor Hugo said, "No army can withstand the strength of an idea whose time has come." But many try to stop imminent changes, anyway.

Therefore, as the new message was being sung in the 1960s, there were a lot of sales of the old needy songs—a phantom reassurance that women's status would remain inferior.

Songs from that mid-year 1966 hearken back to the days of man as supreme. Sandy Posey's "Born a Woman" (no. 12) and Dusty Springfield's "You Don't Have to Say You Love Me" (no. 4, where she will do anything to keep him, and no matter what he does she will understand) became popular along with miniskirts, and Jacqueline Susann's *Valley of the Dolls* (where three showbiz women claw their way to fame and fall into drugs, sex, and booze). It wasn't a coincidence that just as women were getting some sense of authority in their songs, Twiggy became an instant celebrity. The year 1966 brought us the hair-cropped, knock-kneed, five-six, ninety-pound waif who made anorexia glamorous, even before we all knew there was such a disease. Can we imagine there was no relationship between women's new power in music and society and the overwhelming desire to put Twiggy on an international pedestal? Here she was, a teenage girl—who could have passed for a teenage boy—a veritable weakling, a counterbalance to the new power of her gender.

And yet, 1966 also brought Nancy Sinatra belting out "These Boots Are Made for Walkin'" (no. 1), an angry revenge song if ever there was one. She let him know she was going to use those boots to walk all over him, because she was tired of his lying and messing around.

I can hardly believe that was the same year I started college, at the University of Wisconsin in Madison. We had an orientation in my dormitory (Sellery Hall), where the resident assistants went over the rules. One was curfew. If we weren't in on time, we were punished. Of course, back then, not only did we have curfew, but women were singled out. Men did not have to be in at any particular time. They could come and go as they pleased. One of us asked why this was so. Answer: "When the cheese is off the streets, the rats go home." Imagine, calling men "rats." I was so clueless, it didn't occur to me to question this rule. Somehow I remember thinking that there was other "cheese" that didn't live in dorms, so the "rats" could stay on the street as long as they wanted. But I never said anything.

It was a time of social upheaval, conflicting messages coming to us in music and through all mediums. The new way was trying to push itself in, even if tentatively at first, and the old was not about to give up its grip. The new voice, however, would not be stilled. And that was embodied in Gore's "You Don't Own Me." Thankfully, she was not alone. "You'll Never Walk Alone" introduced the concept of female social support in times of trouble. Originally part of the 1945 Broadway play and subsequent 1956 movie *Carousel* (sung by cousin Nettie to comfort Julie after her husband, Billy, dies, and again at the end by the whole cast when Billy returns from heaven to see Julie at their daughter's high school graduation), "You'll Never Walk Alone" hit number thirty-four in Patti LaBelle's 1964 version (LaBelle did another remake of it in 1992 for a National AIDS walk public service announcement) and gave a shot of hope to women's music that year.

Several early sixties songs—all from the so-called girl groups—have the same type of underlying wish for strength and also questioned the status quo. Marilyn McCoo became known for her melodious version of "Wedding Bell Blues" (with the Fifth Dimension, 1969, no. 1), which was a demand for some action. It was, actually, a very adult view of a relationship. She expressed how much they loved each other and the positive points of the relationship. Then she gives him an ultimatum, saying that love and kisses are not enough—she wants marriage. It was a refreshing song after many decades of codependency.

"Don't Say Nothin' Bad about My Baby" (the Cookies, 1963, no. 7, written by the prolific husband-and-wife song team Gerry Goffin and Carole King), is another carryover that manages to show some Rebel sass and strength. "He's a Rebel" (1962, no. 1) by the Crystals was a statement about loving a guy who's a rebel. But the very act of loving him makes her a rebel, too, which might have been the real meaning of it. Similarly, the Cookies' "Chains" (1962, no. 17) seems at first to be one of those I-am-powerless songs, but then you get the idea she's not happy about it when she says she wants to love someone else but is imprisoned by her boyfriend's chains. She was, in essence, a powerless Rebel. "Sweet Talkin' Guy" (the Chiffons, 1966, no. 10) told about how powerless she was to resist the charms of the liar and cheat. But at least she recognized how bad he was and tried to warn the other girls to stay away from him.

"SWEET TALKIN' GUY"
Sweet talking guy, talking sweet kinda lies
Don't you believe in him, if you do he'll make you cry
He'll send you flowers and paint the town with another guy
He's a sweet talkin' guy (sweet talkin' guy)
But he's my kind of guy (sweet talkin' guy)

ℛEMINISCENCE
Girl Group songs, 1960s

My favorite all-time music is soul music. The Girl Groups and the solo female artists from the sixties expressed a depth of emotion that satisfied my personal early teen angst. I could sing along *loudly*, because I knew all the lyrics, which were simple and always to the point. I didn't have to understand the metaphors (there weren't any) or even relate to the content, because love was a future fantasy—not a current reality. It was just melodic fun. It was a time when young girls could innocently dance with one another without fear of how it might be interpreted. Also, it was totally stress-free compared to dancing with boys!

To this day, if I need music to energize me I put on Aretha, or Gladys.

Andi Seals, visual artist
HENDERSONVILLE, TENNESSEE

Angry and intense as these songs were, it was a necessary part of the developmental process of growing up. After a long, long period of neediness and codependency, women needed to get out of denial. Denial, that is, of the whole concept of love being all that is needed, and of some knight who would rescue them for the rest of their lives. Even though these songs show that women were still powerless to resist his charms, at least they were seeing that their situation wasn't really rosy, after all.

Aretha Franklin turned "A Natural Woman" into a classic (later recorded by its writer, Carole King, on her best-selling *Tapestry* album). The song celebrated a newfound consciousness of being a woman—the love of a man could make her feel alive because the woman was being herself. Although "A Natural Woman . . . You Make

111

Me Feel Like" (1967, no. 8) has a tone of compliance, there is also an adult hopefulness about claiming one's soul and finding peace of mind. To Jennie Carter Thomas, the song was an inspiration to find the natural woman within herself, while Mike Shapiro learned more about relationships from Franklin's song.

ℛEMINISCENCE

"A Natural Woman," Aretha Franklin, 1967, no. 8

Hearing Aretha Franklin sing "A Natural Woman" really does make me feel like a natural woman, and very proud to be one! I think women are often pulled into so many different directions—with their children, husbands, families, work, ambition, and other distracting but important responsibilities—that they often lose their senses of being a woman.

By senses I mean the feelings, the sensations, the joy, the sound of our own voices, the scents, and even the intuition, our precious and almost magical gift. Many times, we also lose our freedom to be just women. For some reason, "A Natural Woman" brings me back to who I am, inside and near primal. The dreams that I dreamed when I was fifteen or sixteen come rushing in. For a moment, I can smell myself, the "Jungle Gardenia" that I used to wear. The feelings of freedom and promise that filled my days and nights then become my sense of well-being. The rare, fragile happiness of young womanhood enters my heart for a few brief moments when I hear that song.

It isn't the song bringing back memories. That song got popular when I was in my late twenties or early thirties. No, the song and the words stir something inside my soul.

Something that goes to sleep at times. But this song wakes it up. The song offers me renewal of who I really am.

Jennie Carter Thomas,
professor of management,
Belmont University
NASHVILLE, TENNESSEE

As a forty-year-old male, when I think of women and popular music I revisit Aretha Franklin's rendition of "A Natural Woman" (written by Carole King) from my mid-twenties. What this song helped me to recognize and internalize was that women had their own sexuality, had equal needs and capacities, and that I could be attracted to women without objectifying them.

Mike Shapiro, systems engineer
NEW YORK CITY

Carole King has been called the most powerful female songwriter of the century, having written hundreds of songs, including the classics which tells us that even though "You've Got a Friend" (1971, no. 29) "Up on the Roof" (1979, no. 28) doing "The Loco-Motion" (1962, no. 1) on "Pleasant Valley Sunday" (1967, no. 3)—and you have "Been to Canaan" (1973, no. 24)—still, he's saying: "Go Away, Little Girl" (1963, no. 1). Then you know "It's Too Late" (1971, no. 1), because he's got you in "Chains" (the Cookies, 1962, no. 17) and you're still waiting for "One Fine Day" (the Chiffons, 1963, no. 5; and King's version, 1980, no. 12), when you won't have to ask: "Will You Love Me Tomorrow?" (1961, no. 1). Her impact on many of us has been powerful. One woman recollects how *Tapestry* helped her cope with the pain of her parents' divorce.

ℛEMINISCENCE
Tapestry album, Carole King, 1971, no. 1

I was greatly impacted by Carole King's *Tapestry*. It was a landmark album, but for me the title song had great meaning. My mom gave the album to me (as she did with many of the artists from that era). My parents had been separated and divorced for a while and my father was remarried. My father was also increasingly drinking too much.

Although, at thirteen, I was not old enough to really look back on my life as a tapestry, I found comfort in her words of wisdom about how life unfolds, is a journey, and brings riches we cannot imagine and that at the time may not seem like good things at all.

A.D.

CHICAGO

A plethora of songs with Rebel anger or newfound freedom appeared throughout the rest of the decade. Basically, they can be grouped into three categories: (1) Don't be mean to me, and if you are—watch out!; (2) There's a bright and hopeful world out there, if you only take a chance; and (3) Take a hard, cold look at the bitter truths of life.

One of those bitter truths was that society was having a hard time with all this anger and these uppity women. Now women were even having the nerve to run in the Boston Marathon, with Katherine Switzer, the first in 1967. How to cope with all of this? It's not coincidental that this time in the sixties saw the enormous popularity of two TV shows about strong women who got that way through nonhuman magic. *Bewitched* (1964–1972) starred Elizabeth Montgomery as the witch Samantha Stephens, happily married housewife who could wash the dishes, or vanish an unwanted person, at the snap of a finger or twitch of the nose—all to the continuing frustration of her bumbling husband, Darrin. Another twist on that theme had Barbara Eden playing a genie in *I Dream of Jeannie* (1965–1970) who was owned (or was she?) by astronaut Tony Nelson (Larry Hagman, who went on to fame as J. R. Ewing in *Dallas*) and was constantly trying to hide her powers from the outside world. But even he couldn't keep her back. She was Lucy with magic. Remember that Lucy always had to be rescued from her schemes by Ricky, who would say, "Lucy, you got some 'splainin' to do," but Samantha and Jeannie used their powers ultimately to save the day. Do these shows sound like a culture trying to adjust to the new powers of women? Yes. On the one hand, these two women try to be dependent on their husbands, but on the other hand, they are actually beginning to stretch their extraordinary powers, which they use, hoping their men won't notice they are not so compliant.

My friend Basye Holland Shuey spoke of the impact these two shows had on her, as the two female leads had much more interesting lives than the women in her small town in Alabama. She decided then to have a life like Samantha and Jeannie did—and she has, living and traveling all around the world, working as a teacher, earning two master's degrees, and always trying new things. A scarier version of supernatural powers and women was in *Rosemary's Baby*, another view of the threat to women's strength, this time as she gives birth to the devil.

Anger began to show through in many ways, and the most obvious song was "These Boots Are Made for Walkin'" (Nancy Sinatra, 1966, no. 1), saying the boots are going to walk all over him, because of his lying and cheating. It was the same year that *Inside Daisy Clover*, starring Natalie Wood and Robert Redford, showed a teenage movie star finally getting fed up with the men around her taking advantage of her. Daisy doesn't settle for boots, though. Her method of revenge (or "war," as she says in the movie) is to blow up a house and walk away satisfied.

Songs about chains hit the charts in the sixties. Although Aretha Franklin (the Queen of Soul) had the same tentative tone of the Cookies in her "Chain of Fools" (1968, no. 2), Dionne Warwick, of the "Don't Make Me Over" song, came out stronger than her earlier song and stronger than Aretha. In "I'll Never Fall in Love Again," Warwick gives all the bad effects of falling in love, which is why she will never fall in love again and is getting out of the chains that bind. Though these songs are angry, they still have a strong sense of dependency on the man. She is not responsible for her feelings or destiny. It is all up to him. He decides whether to love her, to take her, or leave her. Even though she is starting to get the point that this is not such a great deal, she is a powerless Rebel to withstand his charms.

She might warn him to be good, as Dionne Warwick does in 1964's "You'll Never Get to Heaven (If You Break My Heart)" (no. 34), or as Bettye Swann's 1969 "*Don't Touch Me*," (no. 38), where she is begging him to leave her alone, since his kiss is like water to parched lips. Aretha tells him to "Think" (1968, no. 7) what he's doing to her; the Supremes cry to "Stop! In the Name of Love" (1965, no. 1), because he is cheating with another woman and the only hope is for *him* to stop; Martha and the Vandellas, too, warn "Love Bug Leave My Heart Alone" (1967, no. 25), since she doesn't want to love the creep, but she can't help herself. And Petula Clark, who made a name for herself with the upbeat songs discussed later, did have one of those watch-out-if-you're-not-good hits in 1967, where she tells him "You'd Better Come Home" (no. 22) and see the hurt and damage you have caused.

Anger and resentment came out but were muted. The song of all songs, however, that people think of for female emancipation in the sixties was the number one, "Respect" (1967, no. 1). Aretha sang again about his bad treatment. Many people think this is the ultimate song about women and power, when actually it was first sung by its male writer, Otis Redding, in 1965 (though it never hit the pop charts then). If you listen to the words, you get a different message: Aretha sings about how she comes home, gives him all her money, and then wants some respect in return. Gives him *all* her money? Is this female emancipation?

Our second category of sixties songs concern the power of the positive, and they sound like the songwriters had just returned from a weeklong seminar given by Dr. Norman Vincent Peale on his 1952 best-selling (15 million in forty languages) book, *The Power of Positive Thinking*. Had they attended such a workshop, they would have learned that if you believe in yourself, great things will happen. If you can have faith in your own abilities, then you can develop the power to reach any goal. It takes ten or more years for many books to get to the mainstream popular culture, therefore Peale's positive concepts would have taken until the mid-sixties to reach top-40 music.

Peale's book was published in 1952. Since it was before the Internet, or even much television, information took longer to get distributed. Even so, it was only twelve years before a hit song, "We'll Sing in the Sunshine" (Gale Garnett, 1964, no. 4), gave us a peep at Peale's ideas. But those concepts really started taking off a year or more later and gave us lots of advice and positive thoughts.

Jackie DeShannon (native of Hazel, Kentucky) became a high priestess for this liturgy of positivism. She told us if you "Put a Little Love in Your Heart" (1969, no. 4), then "Love Will Find a Way" (1969, no. 40) and everything will be fine. At first, it may sound compliant, but the message here is that by doing something—in this case adding love—you can make your life better. The advice is to take action and responsibility for yourself and your own happiness. DeShannon's most famous song, "What the World Needs Now Is Love" (1965, no. 7), pleaded for love, rather than more mountains, oceans, or hillsides. Love was the only thing there was too little of. For Robert Herring, DeShannon's words became a call for hope during a difficult period. They were his source of strength.

*R*EMINISCENCE
"What the World Needs Now Is Love,"
Jackie DeShannon, 1965, no. 7

I graduated from high school in 1964 as one of the "smart kids" who made mainly As. However, upon entering the University of Mississippi that fall, I soon learned that there were many other "smart kids" present. The academic demands were so much greater than in high school, my grades were terrible, and I considered dropping out of college for a while.

By summer of 1965, I had somehow survived the school year, despite flunking calculus and physics. Against all odds I had been accepted into the prestigious and financially lucrative Navy ROTC scholarship program (the Vietnam war was on—every able-bodied male had to sign up for something).

But the reality of a Navy summer training cruise turned out not to be one of sailing off from port with "Victory at Sea" playing in the background. It was grueling and we midshipmen were the lowest things on the ship. The one bright spot had been meeting a coed at a dance right before we shipped out from Quonset Point, Rhode Island. But being out at sea seemed an eternity. My new girlfriend and I did write back and forth.

But then I received another letter—this one from the Bureau of Naval Personnel—a notice of "strict academic probation"! It warned in stern terms: One more F, or my semester's GPA dropping below 2.0, and my NROTC scholarship—and subsequent commission as a naval officer upon graduation—would be history. I wondered: How could I possibly turn things around in my life?

Then, across the airwaves from WPRI in Providence, on the ship's radio came this beautiful song, "What the world needs now . . . is love" (including me!). I imagined the beautiful mountains, green hillsides, cornfields, and wheat fields—a far cry from the gray of a hazy day on the ocean off New England. Could I find happiness again? Could I find love? Jackie DeShannon's beautiful song helped carry me through one of the really low spots of my life.

Robert (Bob)A. Herring III,
faculty member,
Winston-Salem State University,
NORTH CAROLINA

Another important figure in the positive power movement was the popular Petula Clark, whose advice was to go "Downtown" (1965, no. 1) and "'Round Every Corner" (1965, no. 21) because "I Know a Place" (1965, no. 3) where all your troubles are solved. She knows this because everything she touches turns to gold in "Color My World" (1967, no. 16), as she reaches for the sky, asking herself "Who Am I?" (1966, no. 21), always saying "Don't Give Up" (1968, no. 37), which is the theme of the Pollyanna Wonder Woman. The Seekers tried to tell "Georgy Girl" (1966, no. 2) that if only she could find her *real* self, she would change for the better. If "Mama Cass" Elliot had been talking to Georgy girl, she would have told her to be herself, do it with her own special style, "Make Your Own Kind of Music" (1969, no. 36). Susan Voss understood her own situation better after listening to "Georgy Girl," for she believes the song was written for girls like her.

ℛEMINISCENCE

"Georgy Girl," the Seekers, 1966, no. 2

It was a song about a dowdy girl who doesn't fit in, who doesn't even try to look as pretty as the other girls. Her happy-go-lucky attitude only covers up her loneliness. As the title song for the movie of the same name, it had a carefree, average-looking—but large—woman who becomes convinced, through a series of suggestions, that the only way to attract a man's attention is to change her body image. She spends tons of money on new clothes and new hairdos. She does entice a man, played by Alan Bates. Georgy was played by Lynn Redgrave. (Side note: Lynn advertised weight control products during the seventies because she lost all that weight that she had as Georgy girl, proof that losing weight is the key!) The weight, of course, was Georgy's biggest problem. If she had been thin, she could have been any way she wanted to be, even though she was a bit too tall.

After she tried to change her ways, Georgy became the de facto mother of her roommate's illegitimate child, but that brought many challenges, too. It was too late; she was stuck in a situation where she would never be revered as a love goddess (which is all any girl wants out of this world; is that too much to ask?). But in the end, the realization that she had changed herself past the point of return (she had a whole new set of responsibilities by then) is the ending of the movie, which was no ending at all. She was more or less forced to marry a man she did not love, for that was all she could ever hope to attain.

Since my own body was similar to Georgy's, this song and movie were written for "girls like me." I had been given advice from the time I reached five-nine that I was a "big girl." The first time I remember was in the eighth grade when a boy named Harold was not sure I was aware of my condition, and even though he'd never so much as said hello to me passing through the halls, he felt it his duty to inform me that I was "a big girl"—emphasis on the "big."

Susan Voss,
University of Western Florida,
PENSACOLA, FLORIDA

During the sixties Petula Clark also had a slew of hits of the I-will-love-you-no-matter-what variety. In fact, her French hit, "Chariot," was later recorded in English by Little Peggy March as "I Will Follow Him" and hit number one in 1963. So, we have the ever upbeat "Pet" on the one hand, and then the I-*need*-your-love Pet, whose song "I Couldn't Live Without Your Love" says it all. Which one was she? Or was she both? Probably both, because singers, like the rest of us, are complicated people with many emotions.

Finally, the third category shows a movement away from the sentimental love songs, the angry-about-love songs, or even the perky-to-the-end variety. The sixties' new social consciousness brought some Top 40 songs with a social message, sung by the Social Rebel archetype.

Sending shock waves through the music world in 1967 with her number-fourteen hit "Society's Child," fourteen-year-old Janis Ian told of a young woman in love with an African-American man, whom her mother called "boy" and said wasn't their kind, forbidding her to date him. Ian sang of the "preachers of equality" who derided her choice. Amidst the pain, there is a ray of hope that someday things will change.

"Society's Child"
Come to my door, baby,
Face is clean and shining black as night.
My mother went to answer you know
That you looked so fine.
Now I could understand your tears and your shame,
She called you "boy" instead of your name.
When she wouldn't let you inside,
When she turned and said
"But honey, he's not our kind."
She says
I can't see you anymore, baby,

Can't see you anymore.
One of these days I'm gonna stop my listening
Gonna raise my head up high.

One of these days I'm gonna raise up
My glistening wings and fly.
But that day will have to wait for a while.
Baby I'm only society's child.
When we're older things may change,
But for now this is the way, they must remain.
I say I can't see you anymore baby,
Can't see you anymore.
No, I don't want to see you anymore, baby

She was right about the changes ahead. From 1969 through 1998, interracial marriage increased by almost 400 percent to where it is now, about 3 million couples in the United States, according to studies in *American Demographics.* I remember, as a child and teenager, listening to my family members describe their negative feelings about relationships across racial boundaries. Even back then, I did not understand their disgust and would get into arguments with them. Others would say things like, "But what about their children? Who will accept them?" Consider the case of Tiger Woods, just one those "poor, wretched" (as they believed back in the sixties) offspring of an interracial marriage—in this case between an African-American father and a Thai mother. Tiger did have the good fortune to grow up in California, which can proudly boast to be the home of almost one-fourth of all interracial marriages in the country, making it easier to be what they used to call "mixed blood." Not to mention his nurturing parents. Tiger has won more tournaments than just about anybody and he isn't even thirty yet. In 2000 he became the most valuable athlete in the world when Nike signed him for a $100 million contract. I wonder how many mothers would turn him away and call him "boy"? It is unthinkable even to mention it. Janis Ian was right. Things did change.

Another attempt to put a social malady in the spotlight was Jeannie C. Riley's 1968 "Harper Valley P.T.A.," an up-close and personal look at the gossiping of Harper Valley's upright and hypocritical citizens. It struck a nerve, as it rose to number one in September, staying in the Top 40 for twelve weeks. After all, it was the time of the popular TV series *Peyton Place,* which ran from 1964 to 1969, with 514 episodes. Both the *Peyton Place* TV show and the movie were about a small town's surface goodness, which covered up the shenanigans and hypocrisy of the populace. People loved it, probably because it felt familiar to them. I remember my parents used to say, "What will the neighbors think?" Which became an anti-mantra for the Rebels later in the sixties.

From this came the cry for more authenticity, and it was coming through, too, in pop music, as the legendary Peggy Lee showed us with her song that pointed to the emptiness of what we think is going to be completely wonderful. The song caused Regina Bento to stop and reassess her own life.

ℛEMINISCENCE

"Is That All There Is?" Peggy Lee, 1969, no. 11

One day in the 1970s I was driving my car in a very beautiful part of Rio de Janeiro. I was in my twenties, going through medical school, and it had been a busy day, rushing from one thing to another, no time to think or feel. Then a song came on the radio—"Is That All There Is?"

I had never heard it before. It spoke directly to my heart and made me stop on the track of life. It was one of those eerie moments when time is suspended and the "you" of your eternal being takes a curious look at the "you" of your biographical being and asks: "Where are you going? Why?" It was as if I had met my older self, we had compared notes, and then we decided on a change of course. The life that stretched ahead of me, with its urgency and "busy-ness," suddenly seemed empty. But it was not too late; I could still do something about it. Happiness was not to be found in achievements, landmarks, and events outside of me but in a quiet journey into the mystery of life. It felt as if what was background in my life had become foreground, and vice versa. I'm forty-seven now, but the memory of that moment is still vivid. And I still feel thankful for that song that reached across the barriers of language, time, and space to bring me "home."

Regina Bento,
Distinguished Professor of Management,
University of Baltimore,
BALTIMORE MARYLAND

A few more songs complete the reality-tone songs of this decade. Cher's 1967 song "You Better Sit Down Kids" (no. 9) looked at the previously taboo subject of divorce and its effect on the children. Two songs by Diana Ross and the Supremes described bad conditions in the ghetto. "Love Child" (1968, no. 1) seems to be a cry for either chastity or birth control, as it describes her growing up illegitimately and, though she loves him, asking him to wait so that they don't create another scorned child. A year later Diana and the Supremes sang about a woman who had risen up from the ghetto (was it meant to be the same person?) and married an "uptown" man, who believed her to be an orphan because she was too ashamed to let him know her past ("I'm Livin' in Shame," 1969, no. 10). She feels really bad when she gets a telegram announcing the death of her good and hardworking mother, whom she now misses horribly. This was still the era of "Society's

Child," when poverty and color were things to be ashamed of, and it was a theme that was played out in different venues. Ten years earlier in "Imitation of Life," Lana Turner's black housekeeper had a daughter who "passed" as white and was ashamed of her family until her mother died and the daughter then repented.

That does it for the songs representing anger, upbeat positive thinking, and social issues. Two songs, though, do not fit in any of those groups.

One, almost upbeat but also melancholy, was Mary Hopkin's "Those Were the Days" (1968, no. 2). Rather than thinking about a great future, as did the previous Pollyanna Wonder Woman variety, Hopkin was reminiscing in the isn't-life-grand mode of Pet's songs, except when she looked in the mirror and saw a lonely woman. Was it the image of the lonely woman that appealed to the nun who loved the song, as described below?

ℛEMINISCENCE

"Those Were the Days," Mary Hopkin, 1968, no. 2

Growing up in India, we had access to popular American music but it usually arrived a year or two late when someone brought back records from a periodic furlough in the States, and then was instantly popular.

In the winter of 1968, my family traveled to visit two American nuns in Gaya. Sister Celeste and I both played the guitar. So, next year when they visited us, she brought me a new song, "Those Were the Days." What appeal did that song have for a nun? I wondered. Any regrets? I dared not ask. Perhaps she simply liked the minor key. It certainly appealed to us teenagers, though. It echoed the pain of friendships come and gone in our mobile lives. My friends requested it often when they wandered into my room, in boarding school, to join me in song.

Ruth Axelrod,
WASHINGTON, D.C.

Hopkin's song helped Nili London to better understand herself, her heritage, her mother's advice, and the precious days she was living.

ℛEMINISCENCE

"Those Were the Days," Mary Hopkin, 1968, no. 2

Growing up in Israel, we used to have a radio program in Yiddish, which is the Jewish language used by the Jews of Eastern Europe and is different from Hebrew. Every Tuesday night was devoted to songs for half an hour. One song was played repeatedly; it was called "Kinder Youren," meaning "The Childhood Years." Every time my mother heard the song, she would have tears in her eyes and tell me, "Nili, where did the good old days go to? You are young, but trust me; those are the best years of your life. Cherish them! Don't waste them, they will never come back!"

At the time my mother was in her thirties and I in my early teens. To say that I did not understand her is an understatement. I did not know if she was homesick for Poland, though I doubted it. After all, she was among the lucky ones. She left Poland in August 1939 with Hitler literally on the doorsteps. Most of her friends and family had perished in the Holocaust.

So what was she talking about? Did she want to be a teenager all over again? No way, I thought. As an adult, you have freedom, you don't have to account to anyone. What was she talking about? It didn't make sense to me as a teenager.

Then in the late sixties I was living in the States. One day I was sitting in a car with my younger brother's friend, who told me about a song he wanted me to hear. I didn't want the loud modern music. "No, no," he protested, "you are going to love this song." All of sudden I heard, "Those were the days my friend, we thought they'd never end. . . ." I could not believe my ears. I loved the song, it spoke to me, and my heart skipped a beat. It brought back a flood of memories. I identified completely with the words. Here I was in my late twenties, away from my homeland, missing my childhood friends and my home. Missing the Friday-night get-togethers, the dancing in the dark, the whispering of sweet nothings, my first love, the years of not worrying about tomorrow.

All of a sudden my mother's words echoed in my ears: "Nili, where did the good old days go to? You are young, but trust me; those are the best years of your life. Cherish them! Don't waste them, they will never come back!"

> *Nili London,*
> *owner of Speakers' Bureau*
> NEW YORK

The other song that did not fit the three categories was by Cher, who belted out a cry for a new kind of relationship in her 1965 number-fifteen hit "All I Really Want to Do." Moving away from the lovesick dependence and the intrigues, she doesn't want to compete, to trick or mystify him, to fight or drag him down. No, she just wants to be friends. How refreshing.

There were some bright lights during that last year of the sixties. The Woodstock festival attracted four hundred thousand people and captured the attention of the nation. Neil Armstrong in *Apollo 11* became the first person to set foot on the moon. I remember that day, looking up in the sky at the moon with a sense of awe and wonder. All those years, those millennia that humanity had looked up at the wondrous globe, never knowing until rather recently whether it was made of green cheese or not. And here was a real person right up there on that low gravity planet. His words rang throughout the world. "The eagle has landed. . . . That's one small step for man, one giant leap for mankind." He spoke to my heart and dreams when he said, "I believed that a successful lunar landing might inspire men around the world to believe that impossible goals were possible, that the hope for solutions to humanity's problems is not a joke."

As in the case of Norman Vincent Peale's ideas, it would take some time before the truth of his words would be widely recognized.

VERSE SIX
1970s

"I Will Survive"

ARCHETYPES PRESENT:

Wonder Woman/Cynic

*T*he dominant music themes sung by women in this decade were about assertiveness, cynicism, and power. The cynical view came across as life stinks and love stinks but still these are times of fun and getting high. Sex for fun and power were part of many of the lyrics. As always there were still strains of the Pollyanna—women who sang about endless sunshine and happiness.

If the sixties were about protest and emancipation, it all ended abruptly in 1970. Simon & Garfunkel's "Bridge over Troubled Waters," which debuted on February 28, 1970, and hit number one for six weeks, foreshadowed what was to come. On May 4, 1970, National Guard troops shot into a five-hundred–person crowd of unarmed Kent State University student protestors of the Vietnam War, killing four. Then there were the My Lai massacres in Vietnam and the Watergate scandal.

Katherine Graham, the wife of Philip Graham, publisher of the *Washington Post*, which broke the Watergate and Pentagon Papers stories, found herself a widow in 1963. No one thought the shy, grief-stricken woman would be able to run anything. This proved to be another of the century's underestimations of women. Katherine Graham became publisher and gave the go-ahead in 1972 for Carl Bernstein and Bob Woodward to investigate a risky story that ultimately led to President Richard Nixon's resignation—and a Pulitzer Prize for the *Washington Post.*

While this was going on, women were continuing to move into the workplace in larger numbers. In 1950 just over one-third of women were in the workforce, but as the sixties and seventies progressed, the numbers continued to climb until over half of all women were in the workforce. Of the five decades from 1950 to 2000, the seventies had the largest increase of women entering the workforce. It did not escape the notice of some that despite the passage of the Equal Pay Act in 1963, women still earned less than two-thirds of what men did in 1972. As a result, women were angry and started to gain political power. In 1970, the first female was elected on a women's rights platform. Bella Abzug, new member of the U.S. Congress, became known for her championing of women's rights and environmental issues, as well as her quotation, "Women have been trained to speak softly and carry lipstick. These days are over."

The issues Abzug was fighting for were part of the reason the Equal Rights Amendment, known as ERA ("equality of rights under the law shall not be denied or abridged by the United States or by any state on account of sex"), was finally passed in Congress in 1972, allowing it to go to the States for ratification, a process which dominated 1970's politics and the women's movement. No surprise that Gloria Steinem founded *Ms.* magazine in the same year the ERA was passed and momentum was building. This energy also helped in the 1973 suit filed by the National Organization for Women (NOW) against the *Pittsburgh Press,* which resulted in EEOC ruling that job advertisements could no longer specify male and female preferences. The Little League was required to admit girls in 1974, and, in 1976, Nebraska became the first state to make marital rape a crime.

By 1978, social forces were reversing the previous century's trend of few women in higher education. More women were in college than men. It was the year Marilyn French's feminist novel, *The Women's Room,* created a stir with its story of oppressed suburban housewives, one of whom ends up divorced. This also mirrored social changes in marriage. Except for a dramatic increase at the end of World War II, the divorce rate had remained relatively constant until the 1960s, when it started increasing, shot up drastically in the 1970s, and finally leveled out around 1980, and actually decreased somewhat after that.

What was the cause for the divorces? Did working women feel more power to leave an unhappy marriage? Or did the escalating divorce rate force women into the labor market? Both factors were at work. One study showed that for every thousand-dollar increase in a woman's salary, the chance of divorce went up 2 percent. It seems that, as a woman became more financially independent, she was less likely to stay in a confining or abusive situation. Some writers, though, said the women's movement resulted partly from the number of men trading in their wives for younger models, which had the effect of radicalizing the ex-wives.

For every newly liberated divorced woman who felt wonderful, there were many more who fell below the poverty line. A feminist slogan became: "Most women are one man away from welfare." An exaggerated claim, but not so far off. During the seventies, the number of poor males decreased, while the number of female-headed households below the poverty line increased by a hundred thousand per year. By 1980, two-thirds of those below the poverty level were women. The newfound freedom in the workplace, as well as independence from unacceptable husbands, was bittersweet.

Women's attitude toward work had, however, changed. Whereas the working mother of the 1950s and 1960s hoped to be back home with the children as soon as she could, the 1970's working mothers had more commitment toward their work and reported fuller lives than stay-at-home mothers. One young California mother, Debbi

Fields, wanted to start a business selling cookies, but everyone told her it would never work. Her own determination gave her the courage to withstand the criticism and she opened her first cookie store in Palo Alto in 1977. Because of her unswerving focus on quality and her concern for people, Mrs. Fields Cookies now has over seven hundred locations around the world.

The movement was picking up momentum in other arenas, as well. In 1977 a groundbreaking book, *The Managerial Woman* by Margaret Hennig and Anne Jardim, was published and became the first best-selling book about women in leadership positions. Hennig and Jardim profiled top-executive women who had entered their careers in the 1930s, finding that these women made tremendous personal sacrifices (of those that married, most did so late and had no children), that they were more team- and collaborative-oriented than men, and that while men focused on their bosses' perception of them, women focused on their own self-perception. These ideas flew in the face of conventional wisdom that men were better team players, having grown up playing more team sports than girls. In fact, I remember numerous articles at the time explaining how women had a sports deficit and would not advance in companies until they had repaired this weakness. But how could females have played sports equally when so many more opportunities had been there for males?

The gender barrier was further broken down in 1976 on TV when Barbara Walters became the first woman to anchor the evening news on the ABC network. Skeptics said a woman couldn't do the job well. I remember men and women saying that it just didn't sound right to have a female voice giving the news. That sounds so quaint now, for it would be difficult to find many stations that don't have at least one woman as a news anchor.

Television was celebrating working women, too. In the sixties, Mary Tyler Moore played a contented and often Compliant house-wife, Laura, on *The Dick Van Dyke Show.* The only working woman in sight was comedy writer Sally, played by Rose Marie, but she was portrayed as unfeminine. By 1970, Mary got her own show, *The Mary Tyler Moore Show*, where she was an attractive, single, fun, though still often Compliant, TV news producer. Four years later, Mary's friend, a single, working woman, Rhoda Morgenstern (Valerie Harper), who was more Rebel than Compliant, got her own show, *Rhoda.*

The end of the sixties had brought social upheaval and bloodshed, unexpected violence, death, and more upheaval in the early 1970s. It was a time of change for women, too. In 1971, Switzerland finally gave women the right to vote. Less-than-equal opportunities in athletics led to the 1972 passage of Title IX, which required schools receiving any federal funding to provide equal funding and opportunity for both male and female sports programs. Just to prove women could be equal to men in sports, Billie Jean King took on Bobby Riggs in 1973, billed as the "Battle of the Sexes" tennis match. King won. In politics, the world took notice when one of the most visible developed nations elected a woman as prime minister. In 1979, Margaret Thatcher became the first female Prime Minister in Europe. The first battered women's shelter in the United States in Urbana, Illinois, was opened in 1971 by Cheryl Frank and Jacqueline Flenner. By the end of the decade there were 250 shelters in operation around the country.

The woman's voice in popular music reflected and reacted to these upsets in some surprising ways and took off in new directions. As the seventies emerged, with all the unexpected violence and death, charted songs for women took on a different tone. This was especially apparent after Kent State and some other traumas in 1970. Though there were still the upbeat songs ("Ain't No Mountain High Enough," the Supremes, no. 1) in August, the socially conscious peace song by Melanie was this time quite explicit (but still calm): "Peace Will Come (According to Plan)" hit number thirty-two, also in August. In November a peace song by Aretha Franklin ("Border Song," no. 37) sings about being poisoned and deceived but cries out for peace. It tears off the sweet Pollyanna demeanor Melanie had and starts to tell it like it is, as a Rebel would. Similarly, the upbeat but also socially conscious Supremes tackled larger social issues with "Stoned Love" (no. 7), which debuted in November, pleading as a Rebel for the rest of us to rise and take a stand and bring the fighting to an end.

During the rest of the decade, women's music took off in several directions. There was a growing sense of women's inner strength, and part of it meant being open about a previously taboo subject (sex)— for girls, anyway. It also had women taking some of the responsibility for sexual relations. Rather than *her* waiting for *him* to make the move and deciding if he will love her, she was now affirming her own strength and taking some of the responsibility for the relationship and becoming less passive.

A lot was going on with the war, with various scandals, and with the women's movement. Americans were tired of social issues. As we collapsed within ourselves, pulling back from social causes, a new emphasis for women was on having fun. These songs paved the way for Cyndi Lauper's 1983 "Girls Just Want to Have Fun" (no. 2), where she tells us that it is finally time for girls to get to do the same things boys have done forever.

Though the sixties was the first time Top 40 saw a relatively large number of women's songs filled with anger, it wasn't yet assertiveness, with its reservoir of inner strength. Anger and revenge had been the new voices of the previous decade, but those were necessary stages for an oppressed group to achieve a level of assertiveness. First is the awareness that the status quo isn't great. That happened in the sixties, along with the resultant Rebel anger. By the time the seventies came, the anger had softened somewhat and now included inner strength, though it was a strength borne of pushing back.

And push back women did. Television picked up some of the Wonder Woman spirit of popular music when it brought three series about strong and tough women to the small screen. To be sure, *Charlie's Angels, The Bionic Woman,* and *Wonder Woman* had attractive and often jiggly stars, but they could kick butt with the best of them. Amazingly, all three series started in 1976, the same year of Linda Ronstadt's hard-hitting "That'll Be the Day" (no. 11); the Supremes' number-forty "I'm Gonna Let My Heart Do the Walking," where they are not going to take it anymore; and Cyndi Crecco's resolute assertion that they will be "Making Our Dreams Come True" (no. 25) and nothing will stop them!

The seventies produced a great many songs of strength and independence for women. Most notably in the early decade was Helen Reddy's 1972 number-one hit "I Am Woman," which is a woman's theme song to this day. It was, ironically, the same year of the robot-servant-wife movie, *The Stepford Wives*, about adoring women who would do anything for their men and to what lengths those men would go in order to have such Compliant wives. In Reddy's song, she talks about not being able to go back and pretend (remember all those he's-so-grand-even-though-he's-so-mean-to-me songs?), how she is wiser from pain, can't be broken anymore, and can face anything.

"I Am Woman"
I am woman, hear me roar
In numbers too big to ignore
And I know too much to go back an' pretend
'cause I've heard it all before
And I've been down there on the floor
No one's ever gonna keep me down again

Oh yes I am wise
But it's wisdom born of pain
Yes, I've paid the price
But look how much I gained
If I have to, I can do anything
I am strong (strong)
I am invincible (invincible)
I am woman

*R*EMINISCENCE

"I Am Woman," Helen Reddy, 1972, no. 1

*Linda Berger was inspired by Reddy's song
to take control of her own life.*

The most influential song in my life has been "I Am Woman" by Helen Reddy. I used to, shall we say, kowtow to the male gender. Raised in a predominantly male family with an old-fashioned mom, I was second in the line of six siblings: four boys and two girls, with seventeen years between the girls. Need I say more?

I spent most of my life "fetching, tending, excusing, and apologizing" to the males in my family, as well as most of the day-to-day population I would deal with routinely. A woman's place is in the home, seen and not heard, it's not ladylike, and so on.

I heard the song on the radio and was filled with a new zeal and enthusiasm and a new outlook on life. It was truly a wake-up call for me. I felt like I did not have to "just settle" for being taken for granted, or taking "no" as a final answer, or just being pushed around in general.

That line about being down on the floor and no one's ever going to keep me down there again, well, that spoke to me. The next time I heard, "No, sorry," I just let loose in a way I had never done before and it felt sensational. I won my point. I felt self-respect surge through me like a burning bonfire. I have not let go of it since.

When she sings that pushing her down only makes her more determined to get her goals, it gave me a sense of strength. I put myself through school and became a working professional. I purchased my own home and did most of my own home improvements. I became a single mother and raised my son on my own. I walk with my head high and encourage other women to do the same.

My brothers have learned to clean, cook, do laundry, and iron with the best of them, some better than their wives!! And my son is following in their footsteps.

Every time things get a little shaky in the everyday living department, I just hum to myself the tune of "I Am Woman." My family and son tell me if they hear humming, they know I will handle it fine.

My deepest thanks to the author of the song, and thanks to Helen Reddy for recording it—for all of us who listened.

Linda Berger,
NEW JERSEY

Aaron J.'s mother, after a string of bad marriages, finally found her own self and her own strength, with inspiration from Reddy's song.

ℛEMINISCENCE

"I Am Woman," Helen Reddy, 1972, no. 1

My mother was physically abused by her fourth husband, a man who suffered from a prolonged nervous breakdown. This once gentle man became a monster that severely bruised my mother. Such an abusive marriage over a period of years would have drowned the spirit of many women, perhaps destroyed it completely. Never would my mother quit. For years she was bent, but never broken. Through the violence of this marriage, wisdom was painfully born. In the wee small hours of the morning, while her children slept, he would push her down to the floor. She had

137

been down there before and one night she realized that no one was ever going to keep her down again. She kept the abuse silent until she could no longer ignore her bleak reality. With greater determination to reach her goals and a stronger conviction in her soul, she finally got enough courage and self-esteem back to finally leave a sorely sickened, unloving man. He needed help and so did she. Eventually they both found what they needed. This story is about a determined, once frightened girl who became a woman that paid a high price, but had much to gain—freedom.

My mother and father (her first husband) divorced over differences I will never fully know or understand. The marriages that followed could give any marriage streak a run for its money. The second husband turned out to worship Elvis Presley, among other interesting things. Mother was so adamant about having a father figure around that she looked beyond her own interests, placing those of her children first. After a month of marriage to husband number two, we found out that he was at the time simultaneously married to three other women, thus ending the marriage, the title of wife number four of the harem, and finally ridding the house of that country song that drove me crazy by Charlie Rich: "What Goes on Behind Closed Doors." I am thankful I never found out what went on behind closed doors! Life with husband number three was like living in an episode of *The Brady Bunch* gone wrong. Marriage to husband number three lasted three and a half hours—tops! The three children of husband number three did not like my mother and despised my two siblings and me.

The last straw for husband number three was the discovery of my mother's degenerative medical condition. You would think a person marrying a woman would know these things ahead of time. Not wanting the responsibility of caring for her, he left us—much to our pleasure!

The fourth husband started out nice. He taught us lots of things. It was strange that he did not want mother to work. Mother did want to work. She also wanted to be independent, while still married. She was strong; she was a woman. Helen Reddy's song "I Am Woman" gave her the courage to stand up for herself. She still had some growing to do. Her once happy marriage to husband number four, however, became destructive, and that slowed, maybe even reversed her progress. The song made her realize what kind of person she wanted to be. She went from being a manipulative, childish girl to a woman believing in herself for the first time ever. She only needed to act on what she believed about her inner self. During the last five years of her life, she fully lived out her dreams of independence, becoming true to her inner self—*invincible*. She once was lost but then was found by her fifth husband, and they lived happily until she succumbed to a degenerative disease some time ago. She was a woman; I watched her grow. She stood toe to toe with men until she found a true man (husband number five) and lover that could understand that she was a strong, invincible, and independent woman. These characteristics made husband number five fall in love with her. She paid the price, but look how much she gained. If you listen to the song "I Am Woman" by Helen Reddy, you'll know what I mean.

Aaron J.,
corporate trainer,
DETROIT, MICHIGAN

It was a time of learning new ways for women. Many of us were still caught in the old paradigm. I remember signing up for a "Powder

Puff Mechanics" course in 1972. One of my male friends told me mechanics was not for girls. So I never attended the class. I had no idea how the stereotypes had influenced me.

The year 1973 brought Carly Simon's classic song of anger and of assertion, "You're So Vain," to the top of the charts (no. 1). The song was rumored to have been written about Mick Jagger, Warren Beatty, or David Geffen. The man in her song told her lies, and instead of wishing he would come back, as all those codependent ones do, she instead lets him have it. Her over-the-top success was followed by another hit in 1974, "Haven't Got Time for the Pain" (no. 14). It was a good follow-up to "You're So Vain," because in it she tells of how she used to cry herself to sleep (for the "Vain" guy?) and was miserable in order to feel alive, but now has grown enough emotionally that she doesn't need to be in pain anymore. The song has an amazing level of self-awareness considering what most songs are about. Too much suffering is shown as an addiction, so when Carly sings that suffering was the only means of feeling life, she wants to leave her self-involvement behind.

With a similar theme to "You're So Vain" came Linda Ronstadt's 1975 number-one hit "You're No Good." In it she rebukes the guy who lied to her, and at the same time she pauses for some self-reflection on how she hurt her previous man. Notice that these more sophisticated and angry songs of Simon and Ronstadt hit number one. Some nerve in the popular culture was being touched.

Maria Muldaur (who also used her sexual power in other songs, as described later) sang "I'm a Woman" (1974, no. 12)—not to be confused with Helen Reddy's "I Am Woman." In Muldaur's song, there's good documentation of the tension on the modern working wife and mother. She rushed home from work, washed the socks, ironed the shirts, scrubbed the house, fed the baby, changed the oil in the car, cooked a great meal, and all the time looked beautiful for her husband. I remember those days when we thought we could do it all.

Now we know better and that song is almost a caricature of the ideal "liberated" woman. In fact, that song was used as the theme for a television commercial a few years later. Since it was Muldaur, we could expect an underlying sexual theme, which comes out in the earthy manner in which she sings the song. Helen Reddy she was not!

Helen Reddy had another hit in 1975, "Ain't No Way to Treat a Lady" (no. 8, her last Top Ten song), in which she attacks man's fascination with his own needs, all the while the woman trying to love and please him.

A similar theme—I won't take it anymore—spawned several hits in the seventies. Crystal Gayle lets him know she won't settle for taking him "Half the Way" (Crystal Gayle, 1979, no. 15), especially if he is too arrogant and thinks he is "Mr. Big Stuff" (Jean Knight, 1971, no. 2). She won't lie anymore, because the love is gone (Barbra Streisand, "My Heart Belongs to Me," 1977, no. 4). She has to tell him the truth that the feeling is gone. There is a sense in Streisand's song that she is not ready to become codependent with anyone and she is holding back. She keeps saying that her heart belongs to her. In another song, the only acceptable solution is resolving all the conflicts, which is going to take a "Lotta Love" (1978, no. 8) from Nicolette Larson (who had only one other Top 40 hit, a duet with Michael McDonald, in 1980). But, after all, what's the point of a relationship when men cheat ("Young Hearts Run Free," Candi Stanton, 1975, no. 20), especially if they are "Married Men" (Bette Midler, 1979, no. 40). These themes were echoed in songs, including "I Can't Hear You No More" (Helen Reddy, 1976, no. 29); "I'm Gonna Let My Heart Do the Walking" (the Supremes, 1976, no. 40); because I've decided on "No More Tears" (Barbra Streisand and Donna Summer, 1979, no. 1).

The I-won't-take-it theme by women also permeated some male songs. One in particular was 1977's number-five hit by Kenny Rogers, "Lucille," about a woman who ups and leaves her husband and four hungry kids. In the song, we learn she is tired of living only on dreams, but then the husband makes out like *she* is a deadbeat wife and mother. She just got fed up beyond her ability to cope, something other women could relate to. Lynn Phillips understood.

ℛEMINISCENCE

"Lucille," Kenny Rogers, 1977, no. 5

Ican certainly sympathize with Lucille because I had three hungry children and a husband who rarely worked while I worked as a secretary for some of the biggest SOBs in Mississippi and would have to come home and make dinner for everyone because my husband didn't cook. He occasionally cleaned but didn't baby-sit much, so I always had to pay for child care for the youngest child and the older ones were really too young to stay home alone after school while he was at McDonald's reading *Scientific American*. I often remarked to him how sometime I would like to live his life and not mine.

Periodically I would hear of women who just up and left their families, walking out on children and husbands. Although I never did, once in a while these kinds of thoughts would cross my mind. When I first heard the song about Lucille, I thought, "Welcome to the wonderful world of wives and mothers, guy. Have a taste of what we live every day."

Lynn Phillips
HATTIESBURG, MISSISSIPPI

Two more of these "strength" songs bear noting. Diana Ross (having recently embarked on a solo career in 1970) sang the theme from *Mahogany*, a fashion film for the seventies, which established her as an international diva. Questions are asked in the song that might be the same for a career counselor or management consultant. Do you know what you want to be doing or where you want to be going? She tells of the dangers of only looking back and not creating a new future. In fact, I use the song to illustrate the importance of creating a vision for organizations.

Finally, one of my favorite songs of the decade harks back to Skeeter Davis's 1963 number-two hit "End of the World," in which he dumps her and she feels no reason to go on. Here we are, sixteen years later, in 1979, and what is Gloria Gaynor's response when he leaves her? She announces: "I Will Survive" (no. 1). She gets dumped, just as Davis did, and she does, in fact, feel sorry for herself. But then she remembers how bad he treated her and she gets strong and learns to get along, so when he shows up again, she tells him to get lost.

"I WILL SURVIVE"
At first I was afraid I was petrified
Kept thinkin' I could never live without you by my side
And I spent oh so many nights
Just feeling sorry for myself.
I used to cry
But now I hold my head up high
And you see me somebody new
I'm not that chained up little person still in love with you,
And so you feel like droppin' in
And just expect me to be free,
Now I'm savin' all my lovin' for someone who's lovin' me
Go on now, go walk out the door
Just turn around now
('cause) you're not welcome anymore
Weren't you the one who tried to hurt me with goodbye
Did I crumble
Did you think I'd lay down and die?
Oh no, not I.

I will survive
Oh as long as I know how to love I know I'll stay alive;
I've got all my life to live,
I've got all my love to give and I'll survive,
I will survive. Hey hey.

What a high note on which to end the decade. She has grown to a new and stronger person, one able to take care of herself. Kirsten Zemke-White of New Zealand recounts how such songs of strength can help prevent manipulation of women.

ℛEMINISCENCE

"I Will Survive," Gloria Gaynor, 1978, no. 1

I heard a comedian the other night on late-night television talking about trying to pick up "chicks" in a nightclub. He talked about meeting someone, dancing with her, and knowing he was going to "get lucky." Then the DJ would play one of "those songs," the ones like "I Will Survive" where the girls gather in a circle in the middle of the dance floor chanting the lyrics out loud: "But then I spent so many nights thinking how you did me wrong and I grew strong. . . . I will survive, hey hey." And the comedian then said he knew he wouldn't "get laid" now.

Those songs in retrospect probably saved many of our lives. They reminded us at the time that we were strong and that we don't need a man's approval to feel good about ourselves, and they may have prevented us from some potentially harmful (in many ways) sexual encounters. While the audience on the late-night TV show thought it was funny that this man didn't get any casual sex that night, I thought about how great it was that there were some positive songs for women while I was growing up and wondered if this and other songs like it had possibly saved some of us.

Kirsten Zemke-White,
musicologist, University of Auckland,
AUCKLAND, NEW ZEALAND

Starting in the sixties and continuing into the seventies, a prominent theme in music was life's harshness. These songs tended to chronicle social and personal ills. Several songs stand out; in "So Far Away"(1971, no.14) Carole King lamented our society's increased mobility which distances people from each other. The Blues and country music themes about how "life stinks" had permeated into popular music. The women of country had been singing that for decades. Tammy Wynette, First Lady of Country music and the mistress of emotional content, kept singing about life's pains. The song that Wynette reported as her favorite gave one woman hope to keep on living.

ℛEMINISCENCE

"The Wonders You Perform,"
Tammy Wynette, 1970, no. 5 (country chart)

Back in the year 1971, I found myself expecting a child and alone. The father was in Alabama and had beaten me so badly that I had to run home to my mother in Florida. I was only two months from delivery when I went to the hospital at 2 A.M. because my water broke. I told the nurses that I was scared, that something didn't feel right. They told me everything was fine and to relax. But this was my third child and I knew in my heart that something was wrong.

By the next evening, my son came. I asked the doctor why he didn't make any sound. The nurses kept telling me that some babies take longer than others to cry. I could see my son lying on a table to my right and the doctor using some kind of little paddle things on him. I could see him trying to give him mouth to mouth. Again I asked, "Why doesn't my baby cry?"

The next thing I remember, I woke up in a strange room as a nurse gave me another shot and said, "The doctor asked me to tell you that your child was stillborn." Then I let out the loudest "OH GOD!" anyone ever heard.

It was hard to accept this reality. Even after going to the funeral home and holding my son, and going through the motions at the funeral. I never spoke to anyone about what was in my mind or my heart. I bottled it all up inside.

Finally, I found a place to live on my own and I kept having nightmares about my son. I started getting drugs to sleep, drugs to wake up, drugs for the pain, booze to wash it all down with. I hated everyone and everything. My mom was terrified that I would commit suicide. I very nearly did several times. I would wake, start drinking, pop pills, drink more, pop more pills, and so on until I passed out.

Back then we had the old eight-track tapes. I used to play them all the time, just for noise and company. Because at that time, no one wanted to be around me. I was sitting out in my car in the front yard one night, drunker than any sailor in any movie and listening to a Tammy Wynette tape. I had heard it many times, but never truly listened. For some reason, that night I actually heard it, I mean the words, not just the noise. Part of the song talks about looking into loved ones' faces while they sadly place flower wreaths around a tiny grave, and wondering why an innocent child is taken when God could have prevented it. She thinks that God must have loved the child very much to want him sooner, but others don't understand the way He worked it out.

That song, that night, was like a sledgehammer blow to the side of my head. It was like a veil lifting from my eyes. It felt almost as if Tammy were singing to me, reaching out to me, telling me, "There is a reason for everything, even if we don't always know what it is." She got to me when no one else could. I went inside, poured out all the booze, flushed the pills, and slapped myself across the face *hard*. Then I spent the rest of the night crying and begging God to forgive my ignorance, lack of faith, and the awful thoughts I had been carrying around inside of me.

I went to my mom and told her I would need some help. For the next few months, it was back and forth, touch and go, but thanks to Tammy and that song, I am alive today. Had it not been for her and the idea that she was singing to me personally, I would not be on this earth. I truly believe that. She changed my life.

I am not going to sit here and say that my life turned out to be perfect or easy; it has been neither, but at least I had a chance to live it. I can never repay her for what she unknowingly did for me. I just hope that up in Heaven, she can know that she saved one foolish girl's life.

Thank you from the bottom of my heart, Tammy. Rest with God.

Robbie Keene
Clearwater, Florida

Another set of three songs about life's harshness all reached number one. There was Janis Joplin's 1971 "Me & Bobby McGee," about her travels hitchhiking and playing harmonica with Bobby, who finally slips away in search of freedom. In 1973 Cher sang about her traumatic life and being the victim of prejudice because she was half Cherokee, half white in "Half-Breed" (no. 1). That same year, former *The Carol Burnett Show* (1967–1978) and *Mama's Family* (1983–1985) star Vicki Lawrence launched what looked like a new career with her number-one hit, "The Night the Lights Went Out in Georgia," a story about infidelity, where the husband's sister murders the cheating wife, but the husband gets hung for it. Vicki Lawrence's TV career zoomed, but that was the only Top 40 song for her.

Another very memorable song is Lynn Anderson's declaration "I Never Promised You a Rose Garden" (1971, no. 3), warning against expecting too much sunshine and telling us to expect a little rain now and then. I was never sure if that was a love song about a relationship or if it was a direct reference to Hannah Green's 1964 best-selling novel, *I Never Promised You a Rose Garden,* which was made into a movie starring Kathleen Quinlan in 1977. Both the book and the movie were about a teenager's battle with mental illness, as she lived in a world created within her mind. For some reason, teen insanity was popular around this time. Consider Flora Rheta Schreiber's 1973 *Sybil*—the true life story of multiple personality Sybil Isabel Dorsett and the severe abuse she suffered as a child—also made into a movie, starring Sally Field, in 1976.

One way to cope with the strength and assertiveness teenage girls were starting to exhibit was to balance them out by creating popular stories of strong heroines who go crazy. Crazy women with crazy lives was a popular theme in the seventies, helped immensely by Helen Reddy. Her 1974 number-one hit sang about the wacko "Angie Baby," a woman who fantasized so strongly about men on her radio that one day a neighborhood boy of evil intent walks into her room and is sucked into the radio, becoming her forever-secret lover.

Reddy had two "crazy" songs in 1973. One of these was "Delta Dawn," number one for Reddy and recorded as a cover (meaning it was rerecorded by another artist) in 1974, making thirteen-year-old Tanya Tucker a country star. Delta Dawn used to be the prettiest girl, but now she just walks around town carrying a suitcase, acting crazy, and looking for some mysterious man. Also in 1973 was Reddy's number-three "Leave Me Alone (Ruby Red Dress)," about a pitiful woman who roams around town talking to herself. Both women went crazy because they were dumped. The moral here: Stand by your man or you will go insane.

Carly Simon's number-ten song in 1971, "That's the Way I Always Heard It Should Be," was in such contrast to the love-will-see-us-through theme that dominated until the sixties. In the song, her parents' marriage is filled with resentments and emptiness, while her friends live in dysfunctional and clinging relationships. The lyrics are strong, but her mournful singing makes the listener feel the loneliness more deeply. It haunts me every time I hear it. Evidently it touched a young bride deeply, but she cannot have listened to all the words.

REMINISCENCE

"That's the Way I've Always Heard It Should Be," Carly Simon, 1971, no. 10

This is the darkest statement about modern marriage I know of. The first time I heard it, in 1971, I marveled at its poignancy. I think Carly Simon is the best poet of all the pop songwriters. . . . I was at a wedding where it was played as a dedication to the bride and groom! Later I found out it was the bride's choice. Apparently she missed the irony in the song entirely and was paying attention only to the haunting tag line, "We'll marry. . . ." How anyone could miss the meaning of how soon he'd cage her on his shelf is beyond me, but apparently this young bride did.

Peter Vaill, faculty member,
University of St. Thomas,
MINNEAPOLIS, MINNESOTA

Another song about love's disappointments was Janis Ian's 1975 number-three "At Seventeen," an honest look at teenage love the way many girls experience it. When I was a teenager, I liked and sang along with songs such as "Be My Baby," "My Guy," and "I Hear a Symphony," all of which describe the elation of being in love and having a guy who loves you to death. But my experience—and that of my girlfriends—more resembled Janis Ian's, of not getting the Valentines I wanted, or watching the rich girls become homecoming queen and get all the cute guys. Catherine Brown saw herself, too, in Janis Ian's lyrics.

ℛEMINISCENCE

"At Seventeen," Janis Ian, 1975, no. 3

Janis Ian said love was for beauty queens. I've found that to be true. Those of us with too much body hair and wide hips and should I go on? Love wasn't meant for the unattractive.

After forty-four years of dieting and electrolysis, I'm still looking for a gentle man to share my life with. For too many years I thought I was no good . . . that there was something wrong with me, that men didn't find me desirable. Then I realized that an awful lot of it has to do with genetics and natural selection—that genetically I wasn't desirable enough to the opposite sex. It wasn't that I was unlovable or a bad person, it was just that society is so focused on physical beauty, which I lacked; that was a better explanation for my aloneness than anything else.

When I hear that song today I feel confirmed . . . I feel like I'm not the only woman with those same thoughts, feelings, and experiences. That song helps me not to feel alone.

Catherine Brown
Los Angeles, California

As women got more power at work, as the battle for ratification of the ERA heated up, there was an adjustment period that follows Newton's third law of motion: Every action has an equal and opposite reaction. Women were asking for and getting more power; there were more songs about strong women, and, at the same time, more hit tunes about weak and dependent women. Despite all the hurdles women had overcome by this time, there was still the carryover of the old love-the-creep songs. It took a while for the new to take hold, and there was a resistance to the new. In the seventies, the backlash was pretty strong and quite explicit, both in the compliant songs—which got more codependent as women got more power—as well as those where women have learned to use their sexual power. Some songs that represented the compliant backlash include, "If Not for You" (Olivia Newton-John, 1971, no. 3), "Funny Face" (Donna Fargo, 1973, no. 5), my whole world would collapse, so "Don't Say You Don't Remember" (Beverly Bremers, 1972, no. 15), therefore "Where You Lead I Will Follow" (Barbra Streisand, 1971, no. 40) and I am "Daydreaming" (Aretha Franklin, 1972, no. 4) about how I will be anything he wants me to be and feed his love-starvation. But please, please "Help Me" (Joni Mitchell, 1974, no. 7), because I can't resist this gambling and sweet-talking man; "Last Time I Saw Him" (Diana Ross, 1974, no. 14) I gave him money and I'm still waiting for him to come back, and I say to him, "'Tell Me a Lie" (Sami Jo, 1974, no. 1) and help me forget you are married and won't be back. I'm in your grip and even though I know better, I "Never Can Say Goodbye" (Gloria Gaynor, 1975, no. 9), especially when "Here You Come Again" (Dolly Parton, 1977, no. 3) lying those pretty lies.

With all the heaviness of the seventies, the political and social upheavals, there was a desire to break free and just have fun at the party. Songs such as "Two Doors Down" (Dolly Parton, 1978, no. 19); "Turn the Beat Around" (Vicki Sue Robinson, 1976, no. 10); "Attitude Dancing" (Carly Simon, 1975, no. 21); "Last Dance" (Donna Summer, 1977, no. 3); "I Love the Nightlife" (Alicia Bridges, 1978, no. 5) and "N.Y., You Got Me Dancing" (Andrea and True Connections, 1977, no. 27) were popular and allowed people to release. Furthermore, Pollyanna-like, "happy sunshine" songs offered a counterpoint to the social trauma. "Automatically Sunshine" (the Supremes, 1972, no. 37); "Happiest Girl in the Whole USA" (Donna Fargo, 1972, no. 11); "Top of the World" (the Carpenters, 1973, no. 1); "You Light Up My Life" (Pat Boone's daughter Debby Boone's one claim to fame, 1977, no. 1) all offered messages of hope and inspiration. Carpenter's upbeat song in particular inspired one young mother as she nursed her baby.

REMINISCENCE
"Top of the World," the Carpenters, 1973, no. 1

My all-time favorite song was Karen Carpenter singing "I'm on the top of the world looking down on creation." This is the song I sang to my daughter as I was breast-feeding her. If you listen to the lyrics, you'll hear they are entirely appropriate for a mother and her newborn daughter. This time was bittersweet for me as my husband and I had gone our separate ways. All I had was my beautiful daughter, Jayne, who was my rock and my reason for the future. That was twenty-six years ago.

Merilyn Anderson
TAURANGA, NEW ZEALAND

Karen Carpenter's voice singing Paul Williams and Roger Nichols's "We've Only Just Begun" became a mantra for Laura Derocher and a guidepost to help keep herself on course.

REMINISCENCE
"We've Only Just Begun," the Carpenters, 1970, no. 2

When I was four years old, I visited a music store for the first time. I fell absolutely in love with the piano, even though I had no inspiration for this at home; neither of my parents was musical and I didn't have older siblings. I've come to believe this pure desire of a four-year-old sprang from my soul, which, sensing an encounter with my true love, urged me to reach for it.

My family didn't have extra money then, and so the instrument did not make its first appearance in a hurry. Still, I continuously imagined and believed it would happen. Maybe if I saved enough Cheerios box tops, General Mills might run an offer for a piano?

One summer day at breakfast when I was eight, I was reciting my broken-record wish about the inevitable box-top prize offer. Little did I know that my parents had bought a piano the night before. They had arranged for the store owner to deliver the instrument himself and play it that afternoon as I arrived home from swimming at a neighbor's house. I stepped across the threshold and felt *my* piano filling the house with its beautiful vibrations. It was a dream come true. I began lessons immediately and the piano was my passion. I grew to play quite well and was invited to do a solo at a concert. It was hard to believe. Here I was, just a beginner, really, at age thirteen.

The Carpenters were popular at the time, and I chose a song they had made famous, "We've Only Just Begun," with music by Roger Nichols and lyrics by Paul Williams. Performing at the concert, with the audience's full attention, the orchestra and my director fully supporting me, I felt my first recognition of how I might use my musical expression to communicate in bold ways. Today I view that performance as the beginning of a marriage of sorts, the union of myself and music to serve the greater good. How perfect a song for that kind of celebration! Fittingly, I went on to sing and play "We've Only Just Begun" at many weddings over the years.

I am thirty-seven now. My career took a human-resource

development path through the forest of corporate America. But I continued my love affair with music by acting in musical theater, and by singing and playing piano for myself and for many types of audiences. Whenever I neglected music for too long, depression would take hold of me, as if I'd lost my love. About three years ago, I began writing my own songs and performing them in my workshops with adults, to reinforce what I was teaching about living consciously. Songwriting is a new chapter in my partnership with music.

Recently I had the good fortune to attend a benefit concert and one of the performers was Paul Williams. It was indeed another dream-coming-true threshold, calling me to step over, to embrace and fully express my calling as both writer and performer of my music. Williams began singing the lyrics he had written over thirty years earlier, "We've only just begun. . . ." He sung about white lace, about promises and a kiss to bring luck to be on our way . . . white lace and promises . . . a kiss for luck and we're on our way. . . ."

I listened anew and fully digested every lyric Paul sang. The song took on a more profound meaning. My love for music and commitment to my life's calling deepened. I realized that music had been my unflinching, loyal, and passionate companion for so many years. It was I who had turned away, neglecting that relationship from time to time. Now the music was whispering, "Come, Laura. I've never left you. It's not too late. Join me fully and let's set our hearts and the world on fire. You know we're each other's destiny. We've only just begun."

Laura Derocher, consultant and musician,
Chicago, Illinois

Though the sixties saw numerous songs about social maladies and how to correct them, it could be expected that as women started to want more power, they would want the freedom to have equal access to a very crucial part of human experience, namely sex. Sometimes it was for freedom, sometimes for fun, and sometimes for power. If men could do all these things, why couldn't women? Or maybe she could get a man to love her, not leave her, and even dominate him, all while being seductive. These songs with explicit sexuality were mirroring social changes evident in other media, as well. Consider that in 1973 Bernardo Bertolucci's *Last Tango in Paris* became an international controversy. It was a film in which the star Marlon Brando engaged in shocking, brutal, and graphic sex with a stranger (Maria Schneider) in a Paris apartment. The newfound power of women was getting intertwined with sexual freedom.

Just listen to some of these themes and decide for yourself which of the songs are about freedom, fun, seduction, or power. Melanie, who was becoming known for unusual songs, hit number one in 1971 with "Brand New Key," about a girl whose "roller skates" needed the boy's "key" and how they need to get together so she can show him how far she goes. There are a lot of double meanings there. Helen Redding hit number thirteen that same year with "I Don't Know How to Love Him," from *Jesus Christ Superstar*. One would think the song would be pure, coming from a Broadway show with that title, but the lyrics relate to Mary Magdalene and her relationship with Jesus. Mary, purportedly a prostitute (though some scholars dispute this), wants to love Jesus but doesn't know how, outside of bringing him "down" because she wants him so. Aretha Franklin's 1971 number-nine "Rock Steady" instructs him to sway his hips and rock steady.

Bette Midler did the cover song "Do You Want to Dance?" (1972, no. 17), which was originally recorded in 1958 by the writer Bobby Freeman, an unknown who didn't have any more hits. It was Midler's first Top 40 hit and the style was unique not only in Freeman's original, but also in the remakes by the Beach Boys, the Mamas and the Papas, and Del Shannon. Midler's steamy invitation was for a kind of dancing that is done horizontally.

In 1973 Sylvia's number-three hit "Pillow Talk" was a plea for some nighttime nooky, to light his fire and let two tangle. As suggestive as this was for the early seventies, it did not compete with her 1976 cover of Marvin Gaye's song "You Sure Love to Ball," which may have been too raunchy to make the charts. The bedtime bumps theme was also in "Satin Sheets" (Jeanne Pruett 1973, no. 28), Roberta Flack's 1974 number-one "I Feel Like Making Love", and Donna Summers's "Love to Love You, Baby" (1975, no. 2).

By 1975, Helen Reddy was back with "Emotion" (no. 22) which had references to tumbling and filling nights and blowing lights. Were these double meanings or not? In "Somewhere in the Night" (no. 19) that same year, she says he is her song and she wants to play him over and over again all through the night.

Christina Aguilera doesn't have anything on Phoebe Snow's "Poetry Man" (1975, no. 5), who's a genie that she will rub, or Maria Muldaur's sending her camel to bed because it's "Midnight at the Oasis" (1974, no. 6) and her man can ride her all night, or the "Rockin' Chair" (1975, no. 9) Gwen McRae wants to be for him. Joni Mitchell blared that "You Turn Me On, I'm a Radio" (1972, no. 25); Meri Wilson wanted her "Telephone Man" (1977, no. 18) to put it where he could, such as the bedroom and the hall, giving her a buzz until she felt a ding-a-ling; and Anita Ward told him to "Ring My Bell" (1979, no. 1) tonight—so ding-dong-ding.

The seventies were a whirl of social change. A foil for the chaotic tumult became one of the most popular TV shows of the decade. *All in the Family* pitted a working-class man, the bigoted Archie Bunker (Carroll O'Connor), against any group or person imaginable, including his own Polish son-in-law (Rob Reiner), whom he called "Meathead." His complex treatment of wife Edith (played by Jean Stapleton) mirrored the confusion and changing expectations around women's role in society and the family. The anxieties of shifting values, norms, and behaviors were brought to the surface as this show helped widen the topics suitable for discussion on television, including menopause and impotence. If Archie had been only a bigot, the series could not have been enduring. Underneath he was just a regular Joe trying to support his family through backbreaking work. No wonder many people could identify with him and his unease as the world changed beneath his very feet.

All of us were enmeshed in transformation and we were all exhausted. And some of the Top 40 music of the eighties reflected these changes.

VERSE SEVEN
1980s

"What's Love Got to Do with It?"

ARCHETYPE:

Assertive/Sexpot

*T*he themes that dominated this period were sex and assertive-ness. Love is good but it is also difficult. Women were getting stronger through self-help and inspiration. Awareness of the power of spiritual healing and women friends resonated through many songs as women gained strength through growth.

The new decade, later known for its greed and excesses, began with a big bang in March when Washington State's Mount St. Helens blew its top, spewing out lava and other debris while creating an atmosphere filled with black ash.

On December 8, 1980, forty-year-old John Lennon was walking into his apartment building—the Dakota—in New York City and was murdered by Mark David Chapman. The world was horrified. Another day that the music died.

The first woman to be on the U.S. Supreme Court, Sandra Day O'Connor, was confirmed by the U.S. Senate in 1981; Geraldine Ferraro became the first woman on a U.S. presidential ticket in 1984; and Sally

Ride became the first U.S. woman in space in 1983. Ride, who has a Ph.D. in physics from Stanford University, was one of thirty-five chosen out of eight thousand applicants for the astronaut program. After witnessing too many years of injustice against women, Eleanor Smeal started the Feminist Majority Foundation in 1987, dedicated to women's equality, reproductive health, and nonviolence. Twenty-one-year-old Yale architecture student Maya Lin was chosen in 1981 to design the Vietnam Veteran's Memorial in Washington, D.C. Her design called for a large polished stone to be engraved with the names of every fallen soldier, as if etched on the pages of a book. She wanted people to touch the names. Because it didn't have the traditional male figures hoisting a flag, her design was widely criticized. Today it is the most visited memorial in the United States.

The eighties saw women assuming leadership around the world, too. Anita Roddick cofounded with husband, Gordon, the Body Shop in England and became a global champion of socially responsible business. Vigdís Finnbogadóttir became Iceland's first president in 1980; while Norway elected its first female prime minister in 1981, Gro Harlem Brundtland, who became the world's first prime minister to have a gender-balanced cabinet. Pakistan, as India had earlier, elected a strong woman who was the daughter of a courageous and beloved leader—in this case assassinated Prime Minister Zulfikar Ali Bhutto. Educated at Radcliffe and Oxford, the intelligent and striking Benazir Bhutto became the first elected head of an Islamic state when she was sworn in as prime minister of Pakistan in 1988, continuing her father's legacy of social reform and adding her own of gender equality.

Gender issues started to hit the international arena, as human rights and women's groups gained a greater voice protesting against female genital mutilation (FGM, sometimes called female circumcision), widely practiced in twenty-eight African countries and some parts of the Middle East for centuries. To date, some 135 million females have suffered FGM, with another 2 million per year at risk. International pressure caused Kenya to ban FGM in 1982.

And a relationship that would dominate the 1980s began in 1981 when Prince Charles of England married Lady Diana Spencer in what was billed as the social event of the decade, with six hundred thousand people in attendance. It was the first time in three hundred years that a commoner had married an English heir to the throne. Back then we still believed in Prince Charming. Evidently, so did Lady Di.

Women's music in the eighties was dominated by two competing themes: One, the cry for Prince Charming, and two, the growing realization that there was, in fact, no Prince Charming. It was a battle of hope and optimism against the growing desire to throw off the mantle of denial and see reality face-on and true-to-life.

During the eighties, women's participation in the labor force was almost that of men. And by 1989, the wage gap had lessened, with women earning 69 percent of what men did. Maternity leave was common and the majority of working women did not plan to stay home with preschool children.

Women wanted to move ahead. They felt stymied because of the unequal distribution of housework. Some proposed the so-called Mommy Track so women could still advance, but at a slower pace. Feminists saw this as patronizing. If work is toxic to family life for women, "then it is toxic for fathers, too, and we should change the system," as both feminists and the Families At Work Institute said. Still, women encountered barriers, which became known as the "glass ceiling."

Students in my "Women in Management" course in the early eighties were assigned a project to interview male and female managers, one of each from about the same age group and experience level. After papers were done and handed in, we tabulated similarities and differences. For the men, 90 percent were married to their first wives, while over 80 percent of the women managers were unmarried or divorced. It was startling to see the difference. Men needed the women to get ahead. In fact, some articles back then urged success-driven men to marry a suitable wife. For managerial women, though, who were going against expected female norms, being married was a liability to success.

Despite the "chilly climate" for girls in colleges, where studies showed their self-esteem declined with each successive year of college, women continued to go to college at a greater rate than men and increased the level of their degrees in law, medicine, veterinary medicine, and dentistry, and of doctoral degrees.

The new category of cynicism came on strong. A few of these songs appeared in the late seventies but came on as a major force in the eighties. Codependency and strength songs still remained, but cynicism gained. What was left for women except to feel cynical about love and life? It was the next stage after teenage rebellion, to feel the sting of young adulthood's loss of innocence, realizing that the world was not always a fairy tale. "Cold Love" (1980, no. 33) was all that was there for Donna Summer, while Pat Benatar got tired of the unpredictable "Fire and Ice" (1981, no. 17) treatment, both feeling as Juice Newton did that "Love's Been a Little Hard on Me" (1982, no. 7), and falling in love so often that now they just fall apart in Bonnie Tyler's "Total Eclipse of the Heart" (1983, no. 1).

"TOTAL ECLIPSE OF THE HEART"
Once upon a time I was falling in love
But now I'm only falling apart
There's nothing I can do
A total eclipse of the heart
Once upon a time there was light in my life
But now there's only love in the dark
Nothing I can say
A total eclipse of the heart

As a protection from this pain, Juice Newton had to lie to evade his playing around ("Queen of Hearts," 1981, no. 2), Rindy Ross of Quarterflash figured out she had to "Harden My Heart" (1981, no. 3) in order to survive the disappointments of love, while Tina Turner avoided hurt by distancing herself from emotion and asking "What's Love Got to Do With It?" (1984, no. 1). "Fake Friends" (1983, no. 35) kept letting down Joan Jett, and Cyndi Lauper found it hard to trust anybody after "Money Changes Everything" (1984, no. 27). A new consciousness of being taken advantage of at work arose with the Pointer Sisters' "Neutron Dance" (1984, no. 6) and Dolly Parton's "9 to 5" (1980, no. 1). Now we had not only love but also work to disappoint us.

"9 TO 5"
Workin' 9 to 5, what a way to make a livin'
Barely gettin' by, it's all takin' and no givin'
They just use your mind and they never give you credit
It's enough to drive you crazy if you let it
9 to 5, for service and devotion
You would think that I would deserve a fat promotion
Want to move ahead but the boss won't seem to let me
I swear sometimes that man is out to get me!

They let you dream just to watch 'em shatter
You're just a step on the boss-man's ladder
But you got dreams he'll never take away
You're in the same boat with a lotta your friends
Waitin' for the day your ship'll come in
'n' the tide's gonna turn and it's all gonna roll your way

Cynicism was in the air in the eighties, enveloping everything. As the awareness grew that love was not going to solve all our problems, as we watched the fairy tale marriage of Prince Charles and Princess

Diana crumble, piece by piece, before our very eyes through the international media, the conclusion became: there is no Prince Charming to rescue us from ourselves.

Even with all of that, there still were a lot of codependent songs, but they were fewer in number than the cynical ones. What they said did not change much from earlier years. "How Am I Supposed to Live without You?" (Laura Branigan's number-twelve song in 1983, later made number one in 1990 by its songwriter Michael Bolton, where the title says it all); "How Do I Survive?" (Amy Holland, 1980, no. 22); she's given everything to you and all you do is push her over the "Borderline" (Madonna, 1984, no. 10) until she loses her "Self-control" (Laura Branigan, 1984, no. 4), turns "Upside Down" (Diana Ross, 1980, no. 1) from his cheating, and then it will "Hurt So Bad" (Linda Ronstadt, 1980, no. 8). And yet, no matter what, she can still love him better than the "Nobody" (Sylvia, 1982, no. 15) mistress her husband denies and she will wait for him "Time after Time" (Cyndi Lauper, 1984, no. 1), because, no matter how hard she tries, she can't keep away from the overpowering charms of "Jesse" (Carly Simon, 1980, no. 11).

By the eighties, women in popular music had voiced strength for more than fifteen years and their voice was growing stronger. I am "The Warrior," blared Patty Smyth (1984, no. 7), and "Hit Me with Your Best Shot" (Pat Benatar, 1980, no. 9) so that I can put another notch in my lipstick case. It was a theme that continued to develop, becoming more mature. When it first appeared in the seventies (after the angry late sixties), it was borne of anger toward men and all the hard times they had given women. In the eighties, though, the strength-from-anger foundation changed slightly and now some of the strength came with little or no anger. Songs that still embodied anger were Sheena Easton's "Modern Girl" (1981, no. 18), who is fed up with the way he treats her; "Treat Me Right" (Pat Benatar, 1981, no. 18), don't mess with me, "Heartbreaker," (Pat Benatar, 1980, no. 23), and "Better Be Good to Me" (Tina Turner, 1984, no. 5) 'cause I'm ready to throw you out and play "Solitaire" (Laura Branigan, 1983, no. 7).

"Better Be Good to Me"
And I think it's only right
That we don't meet at night
We stand face to face
And you present your case
And I know you keep telling me that you love me
And I really do want to believe
But did you think I'd just accept you in blind faith
Oh sure babe anything to please you
Oh you better be good to me

Songs with little or no anger, those that were looking for strength within, had Diana Ross saying "It's My Turn" (1980, no. 9), "Out Here on My Own" (Irene Cara, 1980, no. 18), ready for "Fame" (Irene Cara, 1980, no. 4) and a chance to prove myself. A cross between cynicism and strength was "(Livin' in) Desperate Times" by Olivia Newton-John (1984, no. 31), which told of innocents being taken in, strangers slamming doors, promises broken, and loneliness. Yet the end brings some hope, as she says she will find some way to make it through.

Even when he dumps her, she finds some inner strength to go on, unlike Skeeter Davis in 1963's "End of the World." Best known for their 1986 number-one hit "Take My Breath Away" (theme song from the movie *Top Gun*), the group Berlin and its lead singer Terri Nunn took on a tune of strength when he leaves her and comes back. Similar to Gloria Gaynor, who tells the guy she'll survive and orders him to go on out the door, Nunn replies to his request for reconciliation that she's got news for him: Even though he had stolen her heart and had her on her knees, now it's her turn, and he's never going to hurt her again. This was a woman ready to take care of herself and protect herself against an untrustworthy male. She was a maturing Rebel, pushing back and finding her own center, as Sian Smith was able to do, described on the next page. This was quite different from the Compliant.

ℛEMINISCENCE

"Now It's My Turn," Berlin, 1984 no. 74

I am definitely an eighties girl. Going through my late teens and early twenties during the eighties was not only a great deal of fun, but also a struggle, in a decade that is now famous for its extremes. For the first time in history women were making real inroads into the upper echelons of various professions and in the business world generally. "Power dressing" was invented and girl power was being sung about long before the Spice Girls were put together.

Berlin, led by singer Terri Nunn, typified the genre of female vocalists singing about overcoming the problems caused by the men in their lives. Often the songs focused on sexual interactions and the use of feminine wiles. "Now It's My Turn," to me, is the ultimate female revenge song.

I can't remember exactly when I first put this record on, turned the volume way up, and screamed the lyrics along with Terri Nunn, but I know that from mid-1985 onward I began to associate it directly with heartbreak. I was in my second year of university (college to Americans!), still a fairly naive nineteen-year-old, and a guy I had been dating for about a month suddenly broke off our relationship for no apparent reason (years later I think I finally figured out why, but that's another story). I didn't collapse in tears straight-away, I was kind of in shock. A couple of nights later I was listening to the Berlin album and when this song came on it just hit me. I starting crying and wailing along with Terri Nunn that now it was her turn, he hurt her then, she'll never let him hurt her again!!!

A couple of years later, another relationship had been going along nicely for about the same length of time (a

month) when one night we got into a huge argument and in
a flash I realized I actually didn't like the guy all that much. I
walked out of his place and told him the relationship was
over. In my car on my way home I was actually trying to
make myself cry—I was so sure that was what I should've
been doing! This song jumped into my head and I started
singing it to myself (really loud!). The tears never came, the
song was all the therapy I needed!

I think a lot of people have a "break-up" song that helps
them get over the ending of a relationship, and "Now It's My
Turn" is mine.

Sian Smith, lawyer,
NEW ZEALAND

Strength showed itself in another way in the eighties: the Prince
Charming myth was dying. You will notice that the gold-digger songs
had faded into the past. So, if she couldn't rely on him to be rich and
take care of her, then she had better take care of herself. Hence, the
popularity of Donna Summer's "She Works Hard for the Money"
(1983, no. 3), which became a theme song for working women. Summer sings with power and anger ("you better treat her right"), something of a maturing Rebel.

"SHE WORKS HARD FOR THE MONEY"
She works hard for the money. So hard for it, honey.
She works hard for the money. So you better treat her right.
Twenty-eight years have come and gone.
And she's seen a lot of tears
Of the ones who come in. They really seem to need her there.
It's a sacrifice working day to day.
For little money just tips for pay.
But it's worth it all just to hear them say that they care.

"What's Love Got to Do with It?"

These five years also witnessed certain songs about fun: With lots of "Flashdance (What a Feeling)" (Irene Cara, 1983, no. 1), "Breakdance" (1984, no. 8), and a good bit of "Rapture" (Blondie, 1981, no. 1)—and definitely tired of the old double standard—Cyndi Lauper shouted that "Girls Just Want to Have Fun" (1983, no. 2), which had a bit of the Rebel, bucking current norms.

"GIRLS JUST WANT TO HAVE FUN"
I come home in the morning light
My mother says when you gonna live your life right
Oh mother dear we're not the fortunate ones
And girls they want to have fun
Oh girls just want to have fun

Songs about sex got even more graphic, especially in 1984. Here we have our fun girl, Cyndi Lauper, having another kind of self-propelled fun in "SheBop" (1984, no. 3), where she goes south to the danger zone by herself. Madonna sings "Like a Virgin" (1984, no. 1) and Sheena Easton combines a sexual message with strength when she tells him she will not be his baby doll anymore and "Strut" (1984, no. 7) around in leather and lace. Olivia Newton-John wanted to become "Physical" (1981, no. 1), get animal, and hear his body talk. Such explicit lyrics don't seem extreme when you consider these songs were during the heyday of the famed Studio 54 nightclub, well known for open cocaine use and promiscuous sex.

In 1985, minimum wage was $3.35 and the Dow Jones was at 1,326 compared to 10,000 in 1999. The next year, however, brought some catastrophes. One was when Philippine dictator Ferdinand Marcos and wife Imelda Marcos were driven out of the country and Corazon Aquino became president. After Imelda left the Philippines for exile in Hawaii, it was reported she had squandered money from her poor country, buying three thousand pairs of shoes and much else. She later denied that, saying it was *only* 1,060 pairs of shoes. Poor her. It fit with the "greed is good" motto of the decade.

By the late eighties things were beginning to change, and the percentage of cynical songs went down while the percentage of "love-is-positive" songs went up. A song that was a segue from the pain of cynicism in the early eighties to the increasing hopefulness of the late eighties was Patti LaBelle's (with Michael McDonald) "On My Own" (1986, no. 1), with the agony she experiences in an unexpected state of being alone. It was as if June Cleaver woke up one day from her fairy-tale life and found she had to make it as a single mother. There would be a period of disorientation as she adjusted to the new reality. In essence, that is what this song is about—adapting to a different situation. After LaBelle goes on about how this was not supposed to happen and she doesn't want to live without him, she finally realizes she has faith in herself, that she can make it. The song is a signal that the archetype Lilith, the independent, free-willed goddess, would be evoked in the mature adult songs to come later.

Though cynicism was the top category in the early eighties, by the late eighties it had dropped to third place. The top category became "love-is-good" songs, while songs about strength and power were the second most popular category. After the phases of codependent victim, anger, revenge, and cynicism, finally we are having more of these healthy love songs. One very popular one had Madonna "Crazy for You" (1985, no. 1). In "How Will I Know?" (Whitney Houston, 1986, no. 1), she is asking, reflectively, if this is really love. It is a realistic appraisal, rather than a starry-eyed fantasy. In "When I Think of You" (Janet Jackson, 1986, no. 1), she thinks of love; "Didn't We Almost Have It All?" (Whitney Houston, 1987, no. 1)—since the love was great and wonderful it was worth the pain of the fall; "Giving You the Best That I Got" (Anita Baker, 1988, no. 3), because we love each other strongly; then Madonna loves him "Like a Prayer" (1989, no. 1); "Just Because" (Anita Baker, 1989, no. 14) we have great commitment; Tina Turner thinks you are "The Best" (1989, no. 15) and she loves you; because Paula

Abdul will always love you and be "Forever Your Girl" (1989, no. 1), don't you worry about other guys. In "Miss You Much" (1989, no. 1), Janet Jackson is rushing home to get your warm embrace and see your happy face; Natalie Cole thinks you're a good pair, she sees the love in your eyes, and she'll "Miss You Like Crazy" (1989, no. 7); "The Lover in Me" (Sheena Easton, 1989, no. 2) sees we have an everlasting love and don't need any others; Debbie Gibson gets "Lost in Your Eyes" (1989, no. 1) and her spirits rise so that she can soar with the wind; "Eternal Flame" (Bangles, 1989, no. 1) asks, Is your heart beating as mine? Are we dreaming or do we have an eternal flame of love?

An interesting perspective is how the largely compliant songs of the past morphed into rebel anger and revenge once it was realized how expensive was the loss of self, as well as the newer awareness that the fairy-tale myth of happy endings was just that—a myth. Then, during the eighties, the songs took on an air of strength and independence about love and made a new category: love is good.

It's amazing to me, though, that even with the new independence this late in the century, women were still codependent—giving themselves up willingly as needy victims. They weren't, however, as pathetic as Sandy Posey's singing that women should be treated like dirt or Vikki Carr's desperation near the telephone. Some of them, at least, acknowledge the sickness of it all. Joan Jett knew he wasn't good when he kept cheating on her and sang "I Hate Myself for Loving You" (1988, no. 8); but still I want you to "Open Your Heart" (Madonna, 1986, no. 1) so I can make you love me. Below, Theresa Jones writes how she is trying to grow beyond her own compliance, but some messages have been instilled so deeply for many, many years.

CONTEMPLATION

First of all I want to thank you for all the wonderful work, research, labor, and love that has gone into your presentation. I think what was painful for me after actually listening to some of the words in those songs was the realization that I see so much of that compliance still instilled within my entire psyche.

Most of my life I spent with the song in my head that I'm nobody or nothing until somebody—a man—loves me. As a woman of color, I know there are other issues at play besides gender. I have come a long way, much healing has been done; however, I can see how much I didn't get done, yet.

The sadness also came from realizing that I am presently in a relationship with a man whom I believe I truly love and he is my beloved. However, he does not want a commitment. I've *surrendered* spiritually to the issue of trying to force love into my life. But I can also see part of the reason I am complacent is the "take what you can get" attitude that was so instilled in our hearts. At any rate, I think I am on the right journey to grow beyond this.

I love him and I know God will guide me. I don't really know what will happen. But after your performance, I feel really interested now like I never did before in trying to understand the concept of equality of men and women.

Theresa Jones,
Minneapolis, Minnesota

Some songs in the eighties still showed how deeply instilled the old value of compliancy was. I don't like being under a spell I can't break and wish I could "Shake Your Love" (Debbie Gibson, 1987, no. 4) because "I Get Weak" (Belinda Carlisle, 1988, no. 2) when I look at those persuasive eyes, pulling me under like a wave, because your love chills me to the bone and I want to know how I can get you "Alone" (Heart, 1987, no. 1). Finally, we have a song by the British Cockney-born Samantha Fox, who had a modest string of Top 40 hits in the late eighties (four of them from 1987 to 1989) and sang "I Only Want to Be with You" (1989, no. 31), because you've got some hold on me. Sam, as she is affectionately called by her fans, was a singer *and* a topless dancer. She is petite, blond, and innocent looking, a cross between Olivia Newton-John and Britney Spears, but with the sexuality of a Brigitte Bardot and the breasts of Dolly Parton. One could say she was the eighties version of Betty Boop: part Shirley Temple, part Mae West.

Songs about strength had very little anger in them relative to the sixties, at which time resentment was the dominant foundation of the more independent tunes. Instead of dependent, I am now "Invincible" (Pat Benatar, 1985, no. 10), because I have to stand and face the problem with the power of conviction. Yes, we are getting stronger, as Annie Lennox and Aretha Franklin tell us that "Sisters Are Doin' It for Themselves" (the Eurythmics and Aretha Franklin, 1985, no. 18).

"SISTERS ARE DOIN' IT FOR THEMSELVES"
Now there was a time when they used to say
That behind every—"great man."
There had to be a—"great woman."
But in these times of change you know
That it's no longer true.
So we're comin' out of the kitchen
'Cause there's somethin' we forgot to say to you (we say)

Sisters are doin' it for themselves.
Standin' on their own two feet.
And ringin' on their own bells.
Sisters are doin' it for themselves.
Now this is a song to celebrate
The conscious liberation of the female state!
Mothers—daughters and their daughters too.
Woman to woman
We're singin' with you.
The "inferior sex" got a new exterior

We got doctors, lawyers, politicians too.
Everybody—take a look around.
Can you see—can you see—can you see
There's a woman right next to you.

Now I have a "New Attitude" (Patti LaBelle, 1985 no. 17) about lessons learned and a healthier way of thinking and I want to be "One of the Living" (Tina Turner, 1985 no. 15), those survivors who are part of the new and ferocious breed. So, just try and "Dare Me" (Pointer Sisters, 1985 no. 11), because you better not take advantage of me. A nod to the life-is-awful group was Madonna's "Papa Don't Preach" (1988, no. 1) about a girl in trouble, pregnant, but standing up for what she wants—to keep her baby.

One song that really touched a lot of us back then was Whitney Houston's "Greatest Love of All" (1986, no. 1), one of the first Lilith strong songs with internal locus of control, taking responsibility for her own success and failures and determined not to walk in anyone else's shadow.

"GREATEST LOVE OF ALL"
I decided long ago, never to walk in anyone's shadows
If I fail, if I succeed
At least I'll live as I believe
No matter what they take from me
They can't take away my dignity
Because the greatest love of all
Is happening to me
I found the greatest love of all
Inside of me
The greatest love of all
Is easy to achieve
Learning to love yourself
It is the greatest love of all

One of my friends used to listen to it every day as she drove her car, as it was inspiring and helped her through some tough times. Speaking of "Control" (Janet Jackson, 1986, no. 5), I want to make my own decisions—not rule the world but run my own life; and I want "One Moment in Time" (Whitney Houston, 1988, no. 5), where I can strive to do my best in the race with destiny.

Other songs of the eighties on love and strength included: We're going to take a "Fast Car" (Tracy Chapman, 1988, no. 6) and go together to start a new life. let me tell you: We are "Staying Together" (Debbie Gibson, 1988, no. 22) no matter what! Because—"Love Will Save the Day" (Whitney Houston, 1988, no. 9); that is, when you have troubles and feel down, love is the answer. So, Lilith, "Get on Your Feet" (Gloria Estefan, 1989, no. 11) and look in your heart and you'll see the answer to your problems—keep looking to the future. "If I Could Turn Back Time" (Cher, 1989, no. 3), I'd try to find a way to fix the hurt; you are the one who supports me, who is the "Wind Beneath My Wings" (Bette Midler, 1989, no. 1); "Superwoman" (Karyn White, 1989, no. 8) is fed up with his demands on her; "Don't Want to Lose You Now" (Gloria Estefan, 1989, no. 1), but I have to be myself and finally I've found courage to stand up; "Express Yourself" (Madonna, 1989, no. 2), because you deserve the best, not second best; "Don't Rush Me" (Taylor Dayne, 1989, no. 2), I need to see if this is really love; I want real love I can "Cherish" (Madonna, 1989, no. 2), not just romance—that is how it has to be.

A sense of strength and independence was the foundation of the TV series *Golden Girls* (1985–1992), about three mature women (two widows and one divorcée) living together in Miami, along with one's elderly but feisty mother. Coming from a generation of mostly housewives, they were now on their own, responsible for their own destinies. They were attractive, smart, autonomous, and, well, lots of fun. The role model for older women had changed.

Although songs of love and strength increased, the cynic was still alive in certain songs. Standing out in this group is Madonna, the "Material Girl" (1985, no. 2), who doesn't care for love. In her song, it's only the man with cold, hard cash who can be Mr. Right. With a song whose melody fit the title, Nigerian Sade (pronounced shar-day, though her real name was Helen Folasade Adu) sang cynically about her sweet-talking lover boy with a heart of stone who was a "Smooth Operator" (1985, no. 5); and while she's paying all the bills, working herself ragged with a typical "Manic Monday" (Bangles, 1986, no. 2), her lover doesn't understand her work pressures and doesn't seem to care; so I ask: "What Have You Done for Me Lately?" (Janet Jackson, 1986, no. 4)—why don't you take me anywhere, you guy who thinks he's some hunk; "Who Will You Run To?" (Heart, 1987, no. 7) when your world breaks and you fall down—you never appreciated what I did for you; Cher reminded us that, no matter what, eventually "We All Sleep Alone" (1988, no. 14); Paula Abdul had a "Cold Hearted" (1989, no. 1) man; she warned not to be fooled by him, because when you look in his eyes you see lies and a cold-blooded snake; in "Toy Soldiers," Martika (1989, no. 1) laments how everyone falls down and is torn about bit by bit.

The importance of the sex category increased only very slightly from the early eighties, but the songs remained as graphic as ever. One tune was clear about how to use "Sex as a Weapon" (Pat Benatar, 1986, no. 28), only this time *he* is the one using it and she asks him to stop—a glimmer of Lilith strength. The topless model/singer Samantha Fox had three hit songs in this group. Not surprising that three of her four Top 40 hits were about sex. In "Touch Me" (1987, no. 4) she's hungry for love and his body, and she's begging for him to touch her; "Naughty Girls (Need Love Too)" (1988, no. 3) and Sam says momentary love feels good but is bad, and before him sex was just something to do, and love was a four-letter word; in "I Wanna Have Some Fun" (1989, no. 8), she wants him to move her body all night long and have fun. Interesting that in most of her tunes she uses her name "Samantha Fox" as a character in the song. In "Push It" (Salt 'N' Pepa, 1987, no. 19), the title says it all; Cher describes, in "Just Like

Jesse James" (1989, no. 8), how he struts around, with a gun slung, shooting women with flashes of white teeth—and tonight he goes down in flames.

Then there was the newly discovered star, Neneh Cherry, born in Sweden to a Swedish mother and African father, who now calls herself an Inna City Mama. On her first big hit, "Buffalo Stance" (1989, no. 3), she openly talks about gigolos and dropping drawers; in "Kisses on the Wind" (1989, no. 8), she turns boys on and blows kisses. Her braggadocio became her trademark, as she became an anti-Madonna sex goddess, someone who could turn on the sex without all the pointy bras and leather gear.

During the 1980s, there were also songs whose lyrics commented on fun, bad stuff, and social issues; "Conga" (Gloria Estefan, 1986, no. 10) and "Rhythm Is Gonna Get You" (Gloria Estefan, 1987, no. 5) were both great dance songs. "Bad Boy" (Gloria Estefan, 1986, no. 8), boys are boys, after all, and they are bad. In "Crazy in the Night" (Kim Carnes, 1985, no. 15) she hides under covers away from the monsters in the closets and on the ceilings. Like Billie Holiday's "Strange Fruit" in the thirties, "Luka" (Suzanne Vega, 1987, no. 3) broke norms by singing openly about another horror—domestic abuse. Written from the point of view of the "victim," Luka says the hitting stops after crying starts. The song touched Don McCormick deeply. His story also relates back to the research that men listen to melody first, while women focus on lyrics.

ℛEMINISCENCE

"Luka," Susan Vega, 1986, no. 3

When I first heard it, I loved the strong folk influence in her work. "Luka" had a catchy, upbeat melody. The album it was on, *Solitude Standing,* was one of my favorites. I love post-hootenanny folk music, but usually don't listen much to lyrics. I can completely identify with those people who thought *Born in the USA* was patriotic, even though the words described some of the worst aspects of the country.

Years later, I heard that this was the first pop song about battered women. I don't know if that was true, but it motivated me to listen to the lyrics more carefully. That's when I finally got what the song was about. Then I realized that she juxtaposed truly horrifying lyrics about her depressing encounters with her neighbor who was being beaten and the woman's insistence that she butt out, with this upbeat, beautiful folk rock. That paradox made me like the song even more. Sometimes that juxtaposition of beauty and horror works, like in Sondheim's *Sweeney Todd,* and it worked here, too.

> *Don McCormick,*
> *University of Redlands,*
> CALIFORNIA

In conclusion, the eighties were a decade of greed, excess, and also of hope. Social change was reshaping the world. Not only were women singing with more independence, but also a cry for freedom was sounding around the world, as Chinese students in Tienneman Square called for more liberty and the Berlin Wall fell, as Communism then collapsed in most Eastern European countries. Women had become presidents of countries and were gaining more power in corporations. The world was changing and women would no longer be ignored.

FOURTH MOVEMENT
STAND BY YOURSELF

VERSE EIGHT
1990s

"Strength and Sense of Self"

ARCHETYPES:

Strong/Lilith

𝒯he 1990's songs were all about mature growth. Women have come a far way through spiritual growth and self-awareness. Lilith, the independent first wife of the biblical Adam, was the archetype for this. Men were men and women knew how to handle themselves in relationships. They took a balanced rather than vengeful approach. A newer trend, however, was women getting down and dirty with sexy and clingy lyrics that demonstrated the sexual yearnings on the part of many younger singers.

Women were not alone in their desires for independence. The cry for freedom continued in women's music, and it also rang throughout the world. After twenty-seven years in prison, political dissident and leader Nelson Mandela was released from jail in 1990 and ultimately became president of South Africa.

This was the resurgence of Leslie Gore's theme in her song "You Don't Own Me." "You don't own me" is what Kuwait wanted to tell Iraq in 1991 when the larger country refused to withdraw its occupation. Leslie Gore's theme was evident also in 1991 when President Boris Yeltsin resisted a coup d'état by Communist hard-liners.

Women became increasingly prominent in the world at this time. Tansu Ciller was the first woman as Islamic Turkey's prime minister in 1993. Tiny Sri Lanka elected Chadrika Kumaratunga to become the first female president.

An event that somehow escaped much notice was the result of Title IX legislation in 1972. A whole generation of women benefited from increased opportunities in athletics and it showed when the U.S. women's soccer team won the World Cup for the first time in 1991. It was a Lilith personification of Gloria Estefan's 1989 hit "Get on Your Feet." Or when my friend Cheri Oliver's daughter, Pari, won many awards as the most valuable gymnast at the University of California at Berkeley during the last years of the century. How things had changed from recent decades when women had few choices beyond becoming a cheerleader.

Fed up with male-dominated corporations, or just yearning for their own independence, women started their own businesses in record numbers. And companies started by women are likely to stay in business longer than those started by males.

The number of female-owned companies doubled in the nineties, while one out of five employees in U.S. companies worked at a woman-owned business in 1999. In 1977, less than 1 million women owned their own firms. By 1999, that had increased to 9 million. Minority women were becoming entrepreneurs at an even faster rate than white women. One of those minority women was Vera Wang, former editor at *Vogue* magazine and designer for Ralph Lauren, who started her own Madison Avenue boutique in 1990. Her attention to quality and design, plus her strategy of focusing on one product line—bridal gowns—has made her a household name.

Within companies, women were finally moving into higher levels of management, though still a far cry from the number of men. Women bosses and supervisors were no longer widely seen as a threat to the existing order. There was a move away from the dichotomy of

Compliant versus Jezebel, the idea that any woman who showed signs of leadership must be a wicked witch or a Cruella de Ville, as in *101 Dalmatians*.

Studies in recent years have shown differences in management style between males and females. In general, men are more autocratic and interested in control, while women tend to be more inclusive, democratic, and focused on relationships.

In fact, two widely disseminated studies done by consulting companies in 2000—and reported in *Business Week* magazine—found that women were actually better leaders than men. Hagberg Consulting measured executives on their skills and performance and found women were better in forty-two of fifty-two skills, while Personnel Decisions International found women excelled in twenty of twenty-three areas. Women were seen as better leaders in the global information age, where teamwork and collaboration are essential. Women were found to be more dedicated to the company, rather than their own advancement; to be less turf-conscious; to be more willing and able to communicate openly. Research-leader Janet Irwin noted, "Women's strengths are stronger than men's, and their weaknesses are not as pronounced."

Skill (number indicates in how many studies each gender scored higher)	Women	Men
Motivating others	4	0
Fostering communication	4	0
Producing high-quality work	4	4
Strategic planning	2	2
Listening to others	2	2
Analyzing issues	2	2

Data: Hagberg Consulting Group; Management Research Group; Lawrence A. Pfaff, Personnel Decisions International Inc.; Advanced Teamware Inc. Adapted from an article by Rochelle Sharp in *Business Week*, 20 November 2000.

So why aren't there more than a handful of female CEOs of big corporations? Partly because not enough women are in the succession pipeline; partly because so many women are in human resources and public relations, departments which are not often the breeding grounds for CEOs; and because forcefulness and assertion (where men score higher) are still seen by many as traits of the true leader.

A growing number of studies done in various countries around the world showed that women are more ethical than men. Results of these studies were almost always the same. This growing awareness led to Mexico City changing its policies. The Mexico City traffic cop had long been an international symbol of corruption, so in late 1999, the government allowed only women to issue traffic tickets, finding that they were less likely to take bribes—called *mordidas*—than men.

Working toward ethics in politics, ninety-something Granny Doris Haddock walked the entire three-thousand-mile journey from Los Angeles to Washington, D.C., to gain support for her campaign Finance Reform Movement, designed to weed out greed and corruption from the system.

As far as the general economy went, the number of new jobs generated favored women, who ended up with one-and-a-half times more new jobs than men. Most of these were in the service sector. But government jobs for women also increased at one-and-a-half times the rate of jobs for men, many of which were jobs in education. Despite this, women still earned less than men, but the gap was narrowing. By 1998, women earned 73 percent of what men did, up from 59 percent in 1970.

All this work by women left household chores often undone. Here was a business opportunity, filled by quick-serve foods and more service firms for home cleaning. But the top performer in all of this was New Jersey-born Martha Stewart, whose twenty-nine-year marriage ended in 1990, just at the time she was noticing that women no longer had time to bake and fluff mattresses. Within a few short years, she had amassed an empire that included a magazine, TV show,

Kmart deals, and lavish cookbooks, making the fifty-nine-year-old one of the most powerful women in America. Before she went public, Martha Stewart Omnimedia was worth $250 million. Afterward, that shot up to over $1 billion.

It was yet another decade of great change, beginning with one of the worst recessions in history and corporate bloodbaths when up to twenty thousand Americans would lose their jobs in one day, and ending with the beginning of the new Information Age, complete with unprecedented wealth, prosperity, and more dot-com millionaires than anyone could have ever imagined. Of course, at the beginning of the 21st century, some of that wealth imploded.

"You don't own me" seemed to be Princess Diana's idea when she refused to continue being a part of a marriage with three people in it, as she expressed to Barbara Walters, referring to the affair between Charles and Camilla Parker-Bowles. Di and Charles were officially separated in 1992. Recent years had revealed antipathy between them and now it was publicly acknowledged. Finally, the truth was out. There was no Prince Charming.

The first part of this decade produced songs in similar categories as before, but also some new ones: Love is good; strength; love is good and difficult; codependency; sex; cynicism; self-growth; social issues; men are bad; fun; and anger. The second part of the nineties produced maturity—a new and emerging category. After going through the developmental stages of dependency, compliance, anger and revenge, cynicism, and strength, we now come to a new stage, a more mature and realistic view of life and love: sometimes happy, sometimes sad, and sometimes downright difficult. Not just the realization, but also the willingness to *air* those difficulties, to show the warts. Here was another effect of the self-help movement that stressed discussing the undiscussibles as a means of emotional growth. It ascended in the media, for better or worse, with sensational talk shows on TV. Some said these shows were an immature means of dealing with undiscussibles, and it would take more maturity and practice to arrive at a healthier approach to difficult topics.

By the early 1990s, this trend had arrived in popular music, examining love's lumps. Love can be complicated if "Opposites Attract" (Paula Abdul, 1990, no. 1). Our friends say we are opposites, but I don't care because "Love Will Never Do (Without You)" (Janet Jackson, 1991, no. 1),)*; when we have problems, we figure out solutions. Disagreements are a normal part of relationship development, so let me see "How Many Ways" (Toni Braxton, 1994, no. 35) I love you. And anyway, "That's What Love Is For" (Amy Grant, 1991, no. 7)—to break down defenses, heal hurts, and to give strength. I want you, "Dreamlover" (Mariah Carey, 1993, no. 1), because I am plain tired of pretenders and disillusions and want an uplifting love, so "Don't Walk Away" (Jade, 1993, no. 4), because I want you, I love you, but I need a little more time to make sure you're worth my investment. Yes, our relationship is difficult, but if we work on it, we can resolve our problems, for "Love Will Lead You Back to Me" (Taylor Dayne, 1990, no.1). One of the most unusual of these songs was Melissa Etheridge's first charted hit: 1994's number twenty-five "Come to My Window," from her album *Yes I Am*, the title a nod to rumors about her being a lesbian. The lyrics in "Come to My Window" describe the struggles of a difficult but beautiful love and how she doesn't care what others think.

Another new category was self-growth. To be sure, there were hints of it in songs in the eighties, but it was a stronger force in the nineties—a result, no doubt, of two decades of self-help books, twelve-step groups, and therapy being elevated from a shameful deed to a kind of proud battle scar that friends could share or discuss at parties. Popular magazines had been carrying articles for years about healthier relationships, more positive communication, not carrying baggage from childhood, and such topics as personality types and conflict resolution. When these subjects started appearing in Top 40 songs, it is an indication of just how much the ideas had permeated the larger culture.

Personal responsibility for one's problems was the theme in one of Wilson Phillips' 1990 songs. Not surprising that this group would choose a song about personal growth. As daughters of famous musicians, they saw their share of dysfunctional behavior. Carnie and Wendy Wilson are daughters of musical genius and drug addict Beach Boy Brian Wilson. Chynna Phillips's parents are John and Michelle Phillips of the Mamas and the Papas, whose drug- and fame-filled lives led to the group's breakup when Chynna was two. "Tumultuous" is the word she used to describe her childhood in an interview with the *Detroit News*.

To exorcise some of their own demons, they take on personal responsibility and Lilith-like courage in "Hold On" (1990, no. 2). They know the pain of being locked in chains, but no one can change it but you, and you need the courage to hang on, for things will get better.

Another star with a wounded childhood, partly resulting from her mother's early death, was Madonna, who became a motherless child at age six. Madonna's 1990 number-twenty song "Oh Father" recounts childhood pain, but as an adult she can see he did not want to hurt her, that he did not intend to be cruel, but that someone hurt him as a child, too.

"OH FATHER"
Seems like yesterday
I lay down next to your boots and I prayed
For your anger to end . . .
Oh Father you never wanted to live that way
You never wanted to hurt me . . .
Maybe someday
When I look back I'll be able to say
You didn't mean to be cruel
Somebody hurt you too

Four years later, in 1994, Madonna had another self-growth song hit the charts, this time at number two. "I'll Remember" speaks of enough growth to stand on her own, of letting go of illusions, and, finally, living in peace and tranquillity. She has described quite a range of emotions since "Material Girl" and her 1992 number-three "Erotica."

Finally, a song by Chrissie Hynde and the Pretenders in 1994 was about authenticity and having the guts to be honest with those you love. "I'll Stand by You" (no. 16) promises that nothing he confesses would make her love him less, and urges him not to suppress his feelings, but rather to talk it all out. How different is that from Melissa Manchester's 1978 number-ten "Don't Cry Out Loud," which urged keeping everything inside and learning to hide feelings. Such a message of bringing the hidden to the light of day permeated the mesmerizing 1991 Senate confirmation hearings of Supreme Court nominee Clarence Thomas. Not only did some of the dark turn to light, but the dignified testimony of Professor Anita Hill, former subordinate of Thomas, gave greater prominence to the issue of sexual harassment.

Strength in early nineties women's music is shown in a song that is the opposite in meaning to the 1956 number-two song "Que Sera Sera." In that Doris Day song, she had no control over her own destiny, which is an example of the external locus of control. Mariah Carey took another route with her 1993 number-one hit "Hero," which counsels us to look within ourselves for answers and strength.

"HERO"
There's a hero
If you look inside your heart
You don't have to be afraid
Of what you are
There's an answer
If you reach into your soul

And the sorrow that you know
Will melt away

And then a hero comes along
With the strength to carry on
And you cast your fears aside
And you know you can survive
So when you feel like hope is gone
Look inside you and be strong
And you'll finally see the truth
That a hero lies in you

In other words, I have some control over my fate or destiny. "Hero" was another song influenced by the self-help movement, for it talks about searching inside yourself for love; then emptiness can disappear. In that same year, *The Joy Luck Club*, a film about four immigrant Chinese women and their U.S.-born daughters, poetically illustrated the process of women gaining their own strength out of powerlessness. A few years after "Hero" and *The Joy Luck Club*, Lucy Swift found inspiration in Mariah Carey's song, in such a way that she became a force for positive change for women at General Mills, where she is marketing director.

ℛEMINISCENCE

"Hero," Mariah Carey, 1993, no. 1

I never thought about myself as a hero. Then along came one of those tests of life that gradually helped me realize how to face my worries and plunge into the unknown, because in my heart I knew what was the right thing to do. It required me, as the song says, to look inside myself for strength and to cast my fears away.

I work for a Fortune 500 company that, while trying hard to embrace the changes of society, still has a long way to go in understanding and implementing the changes that would truly support the advancement of women and minorities into its leadership. Then I got promoted to director. So I decided to be an agent of change not only for myself and all those women who had helped me along my way, but also for all those women and minorities who might follow, so that they would not have to face some of the challenges and discomforts that I did. Life is just too short.

I volunteered to help lead an initiative that rallied over 150 women leaders to articulate the problems and recommend solutions to senior management. And I was nominated by the group to present all our findings to our CEO. That day was one of the scariest, and yet most exhilarating, days of my life. Before the meeting I was a basket case, pacing my office, getting a hug from a friend. I was so afraid I would do something, say something where my style, my being, *me* would get in the way of getting support for our initiatives. I felt so *responsible*!

When the meeting started and I felt my heart in my throat, I did what was in my heart. I named my fear and told the CEO I was afraid, that I felt the weight of responsibility, and that I knew this was an historic event I had waited seventeen years in my career to experience. He ended up supporting everything we proposed. Plus, he committed personally to doing more to learn and understand the issues of women in our organization. And the work to advance the role of women and minorities in leadership continues through the efforts of many throughout the company.

Because of that meeting with the CEO and its outcomes, we were nationally recognized by Catalyst, the leading nonprofit women in business organization. I was invited to the awards ceremony to share my experience with hundreds of women who were trying to create change in their organizations.

I want to leave this world a better place than what I found it. Looking for the hero inside myself made a difference.

Lucy Swift,
marketing director, General Mills,
MINNEAPOLIS, MINNESOTA

Male rappers took the youth market by storm with lyrics often filled with violence and bigotry. But at least one young inner-city-born African-American woman was horrified at how women were verbally and physically abused in rap music. Further, she saw that women were buying into that misogynistic message. Queen Latifah decided to bring some change, but to speak to the *Ladies First* (William Morrow, 1999), saying if you don't act like a bitch, then no one will treat you that way. Her first Top 40 hit, "U.N.I.T.Y." (1993, no. 23) was a manifesto for women to act with self-esteem, to end needy dependency on men, and to bond together with other women.

"U.N.I.T.Y."
U.N.I.T.Y., Love a black woman from (You got to let him know)
     *infinity to infinity   (You ain't a b**** or a h*)*
Instinct leads me to another flow
*Every time I hear a brother call a girl a b**** or a h**
Trying to make a sister feel low
You know all of that gots to go
Now everybody knows there's exceptions to this rule
Now don't be getting mad, when we playing, it's cool
But don't you be calling out my name
I bring wrath to those who disrespect me like a dame . . .
I guess I fell so deep in love I grew dependency
I was too blind to see just how it was affecting me

All I knew was you, you was all the man I had
And I was scared to let you go, even though you treated me bad
But I don't want my kids to see me getting beat down
By daddy smacking mommy all around
You say I'm nothing without ya, but I'm nothing with ya
A man don't really love you if he hits ya
This is my notice to the door, I'm not taking it no more

Queen Latifah (now a TV talk-show host) let her brothers know what were acceptable boundaries with women.

The kind of strength that Latifah demands is what many women long for. In my demonstration of these concepts in my "Musical History of Women" presentation, people report later to me how much impact it had on them. One man told me that the presentation helped him finally see what women were talking about.

CONTEMPLATION

I really loved your presentation about popular culture and the messages it sends to women—or the message it reveals about our attitude toward women.

It was extremely moving to be in a room with many women of such diverse backgrounds and cultures and to feel the yearning and longing for the worldview that you aptly portrayed. It was very important for me as a man (husband and father and brother) to actually feel that longing.

It reminded me of the times when a woman tries to explain something to me and I don't get it. There was no place for "not getting it" in the room after your presentation. It was palpable. You could have cut the feeling with a knife because it was powerful. "That's what we want. That's all. Is that too much?"

I find myself since then working with renewed determination in my own family to bring my actions to a level consonant with the feelings and aspirations expressed in your presentation last Sunday afternoon. Press on.

Tommy Beers.

builder of houses, playgrounds, and wooden bridges,
Ithaca, New York

Gloria Estefan sang about her own Lilith strength in her 1991 number-one song "Coming Out of the Dark." Estefan's tour bus crashed in March 1990, and her back was broken. One more millimeter and her entire spinal cord would have been severed. As it was, they put two metal rods up her back and told her she might never walk again. She said later that the love and prayers of many people gave her the strength to fight back, to endure months of difficult physical therapy. When Estefan sang "Coming Out of the Dark" at an awards ceremony in 1991, the lyrics told her story of being in the dark, how love made her stronger and helped her each step of the way to find the light. Estefan would agree, I believe, with Debbie Gibson, who sang "Anything Is Possible" (1991, no. 26) when you set your mind to it.

Other songs with the strength theme included 1990's number thirty-four "Wild Women Do" by legendary singer Nat King Cole's daughter Natalie Cole, who has admitted in her autobiography, *Angel on My Shoulder* (Warner Books, 2000), to her own earlier years of wild living with drugs, alcohol, and abusive relationships. Cole's song about wild women is part strength, part sex, asking whether he wants a lover who can do it all.

Vanessa Williams finally got some assertiveness in 1991 with her number-eighteen "Running Back to You," where she draws the line and tells him not to expect her to come running. Her conviction in singing the song might have related back to the courage she needed in recent years. This song was the second Top 40 hit for Williams since

191

her 1984 disgrace when she became the first Miss America to be fired, after a now-forgotten scandal. Since she was the first African-American to hold the position of Miss America, it is easy to imagine she might have gotten more flack than the previously white winners did. Williams fought back. Her 1988 *The Right Stuff* album spawned one Top 40 hit, "Dreamin'" (no. 8), followed by more hits and movie roles, including *Another You* (1991) and *Eraser* (1996). Along the way, the NAACP gave her two Image Awards. She learned the lesson that En Vogue was talking about in "Give It Up, Turn It Loose" (1993, no. 15), saying you've got to be strong and learn to stand on your own, for only you can turn yourself around.

Remember Marilyn McCoo and the Fifth Dimension's "Wedding Bell Blues" (1969, no. 1)? She is asking, from strength, for him to marry her. Thirteen years later, Paula Abdul sings the same theme in "Will You Marry Me?" (1992, no. 19), with the added self-reflection on how much courage this took and how she never thought she could be bold enough. Wilson Phillips had what seems to be a codependent song, when they ask him to "Release Me" (1990, no. 1), but later on it looks like a woman who finally sees the relationship is not right, and she wants out. She sees the reality, that this unfulfilling relationship (partly blamed on his "high") has power over her, and she wants him to let her go. She is taking some initiative, at the same time that she realizes her own limitations. Similarly, when Bonnie Raitt says "I Can't Make You Love Me" (1992, no. 18), it is an adult realization that she can't control another person and it is time to move on, rather than "Wishin' and Hopin'" (Dusty Springfield, 1964, no. 6) he'll love her and she can be "Bobby's Girl" (Marcie Blane, 1962, no. 3). Raitt even tells him not to patronize her.

Television once again picked up similar themes. Top-rated TV shows in 1991 included three with strong women in major roles: *Murphy Brown, Roseanne,* and *Designing Women.* Strong women in movies included Holly Hunter's Academy Award-winning perform- ance in *The Piano* (1993); Jamie Lee Curtis as secret agent in *True Lies*

(1994); Mary Stuart Masterson and Mary Louise Parker as independent southern women in *Fried Green Tomatoes* (1991); Jodie Foster as FBI agent Clarice Starling in *Silence of the Lambs* (1991); and wild Wonder Women Geena Davis and Susan Sarandon in *Thelma and Louise* (1991). All this strength was, however, counterbalanced with opposites. Let's not forget the megahit Cinderella-as-prostitute movie *Pretty Woman* (1990) with Julia Roberts, a compliant waiting to be rescued by Prince Charming.

This time period was especially difficult to categorize, because there were many more complex songs than in previous eras. A number of the compliant and cynical songs had a background of strength, rather than being merely victim-songs, as many earlier ones were. When Whitney Houston sang "I Have Nothing (If I Don't Have You)" (1993, no. 4), one expects another "end of the world when you go" song. And, indeed, there is some of that tone. But what is different from earlier songs is her ability to reflect on herself and to have a stronger sense of self when she sings that she'll never change herself completely for him and that she can't run away from herself, because there is no place to hide.

"I HAVE NOTHING"
Share my life,
Take me for what I am.
'Cause I'll never change
All my colors for you . . .
I don't wanna have to go
Where you don't follow . . .
Can't run from myself,
There's nowhere to hide.

And there were songs mainly about strength, but with either cynicism or codependence. Again we have Whitney Houston, this time singing the Dolly Parton song (that she reportedly wrote about Porter

Waggoner) "I Will Always Love You" (1992, no. 1). There is a lot of strength in her realization that they are not meant to be and her courage to walk away. But, an underlying tone is one of neediness that she will always love him. Mariah Carey sang "I Don't Wanna Cry" (1991, no. 1) about her failing relationship. Cynicism is present when she says they keep making promises but nothing ever changes, that they keep denying the love is gone. Some strength appears when she declares she must find a way to let go. Similarly, Cathy Dennis, as the Cynic, bemoans that there are "Too Many Walls" (1991, no. 8) between them, too many dreams shattered as other chances float by while she hopelessly wishes on a star. Two lines away from her declaration that inside she is falling apart, she also says that she knows she has the strength to survive, so she is also Lilith.

A few songs merit the compliant description in these years. Janet Jackson wishes she were strong in "Black Cat" (1990, no. 1), about a cheating man who is also in trouble with the law. He keeps lying to her, and she wants him to change, but she still lets him come back for more. That same year, Mariah Carey is not quite the "Hero" yet, as she compliantly struggles with feeling incomplete and losing her mind since he left, in "Love Takes Time" (1990, no. 1). Celine Dion had two Compliant victim songs in 1991. One was about infidelity ("If There Was Any Other Way," 1991, no. 35), which is strange coming from someone as young and innocent looking as Dion. She did have enough passion to sing "Where Does My Heart Beat Now" (1991, no. 4), about her aching love and endless hunger as she tries to find someone to love. It was emotion looking for an attachment object. Another Compliant song harked back to an earlier hit. "I Wish the Phone Would Ring" (Expose, 1992, no. 18) sounds an awful lot like Vikki Carr's 1967 number-three song "It Must Be Him," where she is desperately waiting for him to phone.

There were only two outright angry Rebel songs. One of them was also a channeling of a previous hit—Julie London's 1955 number-nine song "Cry Me a River." This modern version had Mariah Carey warning that "Someday", after he throws her away, he's going to realize how much he needs her, but he needn't bother to come back to her crying. Both that one and "Save Up All Your Tears" (Cher, 1992, no. 37) were angry at him for not loving her enough and have a certain satisfaction that he will cry now, too.

Social issues included three songs that were crying out for peace: Cher's 1991 number-three "Love and Understanding"; Janet Jackson's 1990 number-two "Rhythm Nation"; and Bette Midler's 1990 number-two "From a Distance," which gave inspiration to Troy Copsy.

ℛEMINISCENCE

"From a Distance," Bette Midler, 1990, no. 2

The song speaks about stepping back to look at the whole of mankind and how we are able to experience the oneness of mankind, which is a value I hold dear. Then the song reaffirms the thought that God is watching us, from a distance. Not perfect lyrics, but still soul-stirring.

Troy Copsy,
PARIS, ARKANSAS

Janet Jackson was singing about a lot more than world peace. She covered sex pretty well with her willingness to do it "Any Time, Any Place" (1994, no. 2); her graphic explanation of what would happen "If" (1993, no. 4) he got undressed; and her explanation of how her burning desire as he reaches out for her body all night long is, well, "That's the Way Love Goes" (1993, no. 1). Other songs describing sex, most of them quite graphic, included Madonna's "Erotica" (1992, no. 3) and Paula Abdul's "Vibeology" (1993, no. 16); "I Wanna Be Down" (Brandy, 1994, no. 7); "Let's Talk About Sex" (Salt 'N' Pepa, 1991, no. 13); and "I'm Your Baby Tonight" (Whitney Houston, 1990, no. 1), which talks about the ecstasy of her first time. "All I Wanna Do

Is Make Love to You" (Heart, 1990, no. 2) on "My Side of the Bed" (Susanna Hoffs, 1991, no. 30) and you can "Touch Me All Night Long" (Cathy Dennis, 1991, no. 2), because "Damn I Wish I Was Your Lover" (Sophie B. Watkins, 1992, no. 5), where she offers to rock him all night long and invites him to come inside her, uh, jungle book. Were these songs about having fun? Some of them, yes, but I also believe there is the wish to shock and titillate, in order to get attention to sell records. Women made themselves sexual objects for monetary gain. They marginalized themselves willingly as sexual compliants.

FIRST HALF OF NINETIES REVISITED

In revisiting the nineties there were real horrors: bombs on airplanes; the Unibomber; the bombings in Oklahoma City, at the Atlanta Olympics, and at U.S. Embassies in Africa; the blow-up of Branch Davidian; and the assassination of Israel's Yitzak Rabin. The militant Islamic Taliban took control of Afghanistan in 1996 and began campaigns of ethnic cleansing and female righteousness. The Taliban closed girls' schools and forbade women to work, or even leave home without a man to escort her. Eleanor Smeal and the feminist majority later took on the subjugation of women in Afghanistan as one of their causes.

As Dickens said in *A Tale of Two Cities*, "It was the best of times, it was the worst of times." Tremendous highs and lows were seen in the first part of the nineties, making way for the last few years before the new millennium, after which some groups expected the world to end.

How do you get through turbulent times? With strength, and that was the category of most of the songs in the late nineties. Tests and difficulties can be wonderful agents for growth, making the soul and spirit stronger. We see a relatively high number of songs about self-reflection and self-growth, as well as a new category of spiritual awareness and spiritual growth, with the ranking of themes as follows, beginning with the most prevalent: strength, cynicism, love is good, sex, love is good and difficult, codependence, spirituality, self-growth, social issues, you'll regret it when I'm gone, friendship, and fun.

The late nineties was the first time songs about strength outnumbered the other categories. There would still be enough Compliant and needy songs, such as "How Do I Live" without you (LeAnn Rimes, 1997, no. 2; also sung by Trisha Yearwood)—"I Want to Come Over" (Melissa Etheridge, 1996, no, 22)—I can't help myself, let me sneak in; Don't "Let Go" (En Vogue, 1997, no. 2) because I am miserable without you; since you are "Missing" (Everything but the Girl, 1996, no. 2) I can't go on; even though you left, I will always love you and you know you can always come back to "The Arms of the One Who Loves You" (Escape, 1998, no. 7)—please come back and "Un-Break My Heart"(Toni Braxton, 1996, no. 1). Yes, I know it is wrong to love you, but you are "My All" (Mariah Carey, 1998, no. 1). Listen, "Have You Ever" (Brandy, 1999, no. 1) loved intensely and wished he cared and would be the "Angel of Mine" (Monica, 1999, no. 1), where each breath I take is for his love?

Recall Skeeter Davis's "End of the World" and the he-dumped-me-1-can't-go-on theme? It comes back again with some of the above, including Toni Braxton's "Un-Break My Heart" in 1996. Interestingly, even though the song reeks of compliant codependence, it became a source of strength for one woman, as she named her pain, found her own courage and created a new life. The difference with her was that she was praying to God for strength, rather than asking her man to fix her.

ℛEMINISCENCE

"Un-Break My Heart," Toni Braxton, 1996 no. 21

I was married to a man who did not work and did not do much cooking or housework. He was also emotionally and physically abusive. At times I worked two jobs to support the family, while he watched television.

To me marriage was forever, and I was in pain, believing

that my only refuge was death; however, I had to live and raise our two children. I felt that for some reason God had abandoned me. There were many nights that I cried and asked God to change my life. Finally, after nineteen years of painful marriage, I left and started a new life for me and my children. Tony Braxton's "Un-Break My Heart" is my song. It's the one I sang many times with teary eyes, asking God to come back and hold me, to come back and unbreak my heart, and to bring back joy to my life.

Thank God, my children are much happier now. Now when I hear "Un-Break My Heart" I smile, because those nights are back when I hold God beside me.

Gisso Ahadi,
DENVER, COLORADO

This is an example of overcoming pretty intense codependence. As this reminiscence shows, in balance, Lilith strength comes out as the winner with songs about survival, gender roles, learning from pain, healthy boundaries, and equality with men.

Remember the gender role songs of the fifties and sixties? I enjoy being a girl, with lace and cream on my face, and I want a caveman for a boyfriend. By the late nineties, women had gained enough inner strength to question those roles. Shania Twain has fun with sex-role stereotypes, saying "Any Man of Mine" (1995, no. 31) better love me even if I'm ugly, my dress is too tight, or if I burn the dinner.

The music group "No Doubt" takes a sarcastic view of gender roles, saying don't worry about giving me rights and I won't worry about your rules of thumb, let me take the pink ribbon off my eyes, 'cause I'm "Just a Girl" (1996, no. 23). Jo Dee Messina, too, is tired of being in an inferior position, not willing to take back the man she loves (though it hurts her greatly) because she wants to be in an equal relationship with a man who will "Stand Beside Me" (1999, no. 34), not in front or behind.

Letting him know what she expects and not taking mistreatment anymore is what Lauryn Hill does in "Doo Wop That Thing" (1998, no. 1), what 702 (that's the name of a group) does in "Get It Together" (1997, no. 10), and what Monica does in "First Night" (1997, no. 1)— all songs with Lilith strength. Lauryn Hill's songs became an inspiration for many women, including Kecia Thomas.

ℛEMINISCENCE

"To Zion," Lauryn Hill, 1999, no. 40

In her song, Lauryn Hill talks about how when her career was taking off she discovered that she was pregnant. Friends told her to use her head, but she chose instead to follow her heart. She goes on to sing about how now her world revolves around her young son, Zion, and how happy she is.

This song came out when I was an assistant professor and new mom. My husband and I had tried hard to have a child and when we finally had our son, I discovered how "family unfriendly" my department really was. Yet I persevered, loved motherhood, got tenure, and have just had my second child—a girl this time—eleven weeks ago today. The first time I heard the song "Zion" was when I had just parked on campus and was about to walk to my office. I wasn't thrilled to be going to work that day and would have preferred to be home with my infant son. After hearing the entire song played I felt empowered and comforted by Lauryn's and my own decision to pursue motherhood as well as a career.

Kecia Thomas, psychology professor,
University of Georgia, Athens
ATHENS, GEORGIA

Surviving after pain is what Madonna will do, "You'll See" (1995, no. 6), as Cher learns to "Believe" (1999, no. 3) in her own strength and ability to go on, even though no one believed she could: "Wrong Again" (Martina McBride, 1999, no. 36). After the heartache, though, "You Learn" (Alanis Morissette, 1996, no. 6).

"You Learn"
You live you learn, you love you learn
You cry you learn, you lose you learn
You bleed you learn, you scream you learn

Making a new life for herself after abuse and pain is what Tina Turner did as well as anyone. Her 1993 number-nine, "I Don't Wanna Fight," told us where she wanted to go after all those years of domestic violence. After she left the batterer Ike Turner, everyone thought she would fade from the music scene, but she proved them wrong, coming out with one hit after another. In 2000, she launched her final (or is it?) tour, labeled "Twenty-four-Seven," to sell-out crowds. At age sixty-one, she ended up firing the first group of tour dancers because they couldn't keep up with her. She is a role model of the New Woman—a Wonder Woman—of this era. As she said, "I will never give in to old age until I become old. And I'm not old yet!"

Movies reflected this show of strength in women. We experienced Jodie Foster's potency and transformation as an astrophysicist in *Contact* (1997), Frances McDormand's brilliant police work in *Fargo* (1996); Meg Ryan as military super-leader in *Courage under Fire* (1996); Susan Sarandon as Lilith spirit in *Dead Man Walking* (1995). But, as always, there is still the remnant of compliant, as shown through Emily Watson, the wife who would sell her body and destroy herself to please her husband, in *Breaking the Waves* (1996) and the guilt-ridden compliant wife Meryl Streep in *Bridges of Madison County* (1995).

The newfound strength wouldn't be subdued, and it was also chronicled in a TV series, *Xena: Warrior Princess,* which aired new shows from 1995 to 2001 and was rated number one amongst first-run syndicated dramas for four years. Seen in 115 countries, it captured the archetype of Wonder Woman, as Xena traveled the ancient imaginary lands with her sidekick, Gabrielle, rescuing the powerless, even as they battled their own inner demons. The series was unique in its exploration of the inner self of an action hero.

My grandmother used to tell me how much she envied my life and all the chances for education and travel that she never had. The opportunities for my three daughters are even greater than those I had. They fly around the world more than I traveled as a child—the seventeen miles between our home in Pewaukee and Milwaukee. Singing about new worlds and opportunities for young women to become their own Wonder Woman, the Dixie Chicks have "Wide Open Spaces" (1999, no. 1)—room to grow and make their own mistakes. But these wide-open spaces were not as hospitable to one male, at least, who found himself having women for bosses.

*R*EMINISCENCE

"Wide Open Spaces," Dixie Chicks, 1999, no. 1

A song that affected my life very much, but not in the way you might expect, was "Wide Open Spaces." My oldest son, Scott, was the drummer for the Dixie Chicks when this song was recorded. He left them three months before this record became number one. I tried to get him to stay, but he'd never played with an all-girl group before and found it difficult to take orders from women. Of course, now he wishes he'd listened to his ole mom, but it's all water under the bridge. He has gone on to be successful, with the Dale

Watson Band, but I'm sure being with a number-one group would have fit his plans a little better. One never knows the future, and I guess it's a good thing. Every time I hear "Wide Open Spaces," I think of what could have been for him.

Bettye Matthews,
owner of vintage and reproduction
clothing business,
BONHAM, TEXAS

Strength appeared, as well, in a new venue for women's music. Canadian rising star Sarah McLachlan, with a number of Grammies and platinum records of her own, got tired of women being marginalized in music. She and others reported the difficulty in getting radio airtime back in the early nineties, when disk jockeys were loath to put more than one woman's song in each thirty-minute segment, lest the show be seen as too feminine. When her album "Fumbling Towards Ecstasy" came out in 1994, she tried to get more radio play. The stations told her they couldn't play her because they already had a female on their playlist. In this case, it was Tori Amos. McLachlan saw it as marginalizing, because their music is so different. Her anger was compounded that same year when she was ready to tour for her new album, and wanted to team up with American Paula Cole. She got stonewalled. Promoters matter-of-factly told her that the idea of two women touring together was ridiculous and they didn't want to even hear about it. Not being a Compliant, but rather someone with strength, she and Cole toured together anyway and had great success. That gave her another idea. In order to further show that women together *could* sell records and concert tickets, she began the burdensome task of organizing dozens of female singers and groups to become part of the 1996-launched Lilith Tour.

McLachlan's concert tour idea took off. Four years, 139 shows, and $60 million later—including $4 million donated to women's shelters and charities—McLachlan had proven the skeptics wrong.

•   •   •

Though less prevalent than in the previous decade, cynical songs show that women are still recovering from centuries of denial. The nineties version of cynicism, though, is moving toward a more realistic view of difficult relationships. Bitterness is there, but the eyes are more wide open. He took her for granted and played his lines so well that Madonna tells him to "Take a Bow" (1995, no. 1). Life is difficult, sometimes because he is "Insensitive" (Jann Arden, 1996, no. 12), or because I wonder "If It Makes You Happy" (Sheryl Crow, 1997, no. 10), why you are still sad? Paula Cole looks around and wonders what happened to the decent guys, asking "Where Have All the Cowboys Gone?" (1997, no. 8).

"WHERE HAVE ALL THE COWBOYS GONE?"
Where is my John Wayne?
Where is my prairie son?
Where is my happy ending?
Where have all the cowboys gone? . . .
We finally sold the Chevy when we had another baby
And you took that job in Tennessee
You made friends at the farm
You joined them at the bar
Most every single day of the week
I will wash the dishes, while you go have a beer

Though anger was not as prominent as in the sixties and seventies, it still came out with force. A new singer broke into the limelight in 1995 with a whole album (*Jagged Little Pill*) of angry Rebel tunes, several of which hit the charts. Alanis Morissette's "You Oughta Know" (1995, no. 13) was one of the most talked about songs that year. It was addressed to a Mr. Duplicity, a former boyfriend, who quickly replaced her. Did the new love know how many times he had told her (the singer) he would hold her until he died? But he was still alive. A New York City woman related to the song, and it helped her leave the past behind.

ℛEMINISCENCE

"You Oughta Know," Alanis Morissette, 1995, no. 13

I remember not only when I first heard "You Oughta Know," but also where I bought the CD. I had recently been dumped by this guy who I thought I was certainly going to marry. He had pursued me and taken me to meet his entire family, who welcomed me completely. How unbelievably perfect! Then one day out of the blue he calls and says that he is tired. That's about it. He ended up going back to an old girlfriend—the one he swore he didn't care for.

So when I heard that song I felt that she captured perfectly the anger and hurt I was feeling at the time. It was like she was saying all the things I was not allowed to say. This song expressed *everything* I was feeling—it was like she was expressing and *admitting* all the ugly things and feelings that had been running through my mind for a long time. I listened to the song many times. I even thought about sending him a copy, but the song helped me validate my anger and then *move on*!

Sally Roman,
New York City

My friend, Gina Mendello, went to a concert Morissette gave right after the release of *Jagged Little Pill.* At the concert, Gina said, women aged from late teens through to late thirties were standing up shaking their fists with the music. Morissette articulated the frustrations and fury these women had lived and now they had a chance to express it en masse.

A matured version of the older theme of sentimental love songs suggests that love is good. This theme shows the bliss of love in "This Kiss" (Faith Hill, 1998, no. 7) from "Diggin' on You" (TLC, 1995, no. 5) and lets me know "My Heart Will Go On" (Celine Dion, 1998, no. 1) and that "I Love You Always Forever" (Donna Lewis, 1996, no. 2). These last two songs got so much airplay I couldn't stand them after a while. Even now, I have to turn the radio off if they play. What I learned from them is that I don't have to listen to them endlessly.

Life might be wonderful, but it sure is a lot of work, so if you "Give Me One Reason" (Tracy Chapman, 1996, no. 3), I'll come back and we can resolve our problems, that is, if you "Wannabe" (Spice Girls, 1997, no. 1) my lover, because as far as I am concerned we've come far and "You're Still the One" (Shania Twain, 1998, no. 2). But let me warn you, unless you speak openly about your feelings to me, my love will be lost ("No, No, No," Destiny's Child, 1996, no. 3).

The need to titillate and shock became stronger in these last five years of the century, with songs about the bimbo "Barbie Girl" (Aqua, 1997, no. 7) and her desire to be touched there and undressed anywhere, the "Honey" (Mariah Carey, 1997, no. 1) of your love that makes me addicted—or in the oft-played "Genie in a Bottle," with Christina Aguilera's baby-voiced song yearning to be rubbed so his dreams will come true, or maybe the baby-faced Britney Spears asking to hit me "Baby One More Time" (1999, no. 1) and show her how you want it, because she is so lonely it's killing her.

Taking the prize as most graphic was the disdain in "Short Dick Man" (20 Fingers, featuring Gillette, 1995, no. 14), because she doesn't want no teeny-weeny shriveled thing on him for which he needs a tweezers to put it away.

As the shock value of the sex songs got stronger, it looked more like there was a new kind of oppression. Instead of the old rule about not saying or doing anything sexual, in the late nineties it was just the opposite. In fact, it was hard to get anywhere unless you made yourself a sex object.

The biggest shift in the nineties, which developed further in the last five years, was that of self-reflection and then spiritual awareness, with seventeen songs dealing with this theme hitting the Top 40 charts. Being aware of one's own feelings and not projecting them onto someone else is a strength and is what you do when you "Don't Take It" personally (Monica, 1995, no. 2); the self-help movement also stresses "letting go," which is embodied in "The Power of Good-bye" (Madonna, 1998, no. 11).

"THE POWER OF GOOD-BYE"
Your heart is not open so I must go
The spell has been broken, I loved you so
Freedom comes when you learn to let go
Creation comes when you learn to say no

You were my lesson I had to learn
I was your fortress you had to burn
Pain is a warning that something's wrong

Sheryl Crow wonders why she's a stranger in her own life in "Everyday Is a Winding Road" (1997, no. 11). With an unopen heart you are "Frozen" (Madonna, 1998, no. 2), while an enlightened perception becomes: "You're Easy on the Eyes" (Terry Clark, 1998, no. 40), where, as in previous eras, she is drawn by his charm, but now she sees reality more clearly and has the courage to say good-bye.

"YOU'RE EASY ON THE EYES"
You're easy on the eyes
Hard on the heart
You look so good but the way things look ain't the way they are
Better say goodbye before we go too far
Cause now I realize you're easy on the eyes
Hard on the heart

Songs with spirituality included the All Saints "Never Ever" (1998, no. 4), which spoke of communication, peace of mind, and soul-searching. But if God was "One of Us" (Joan Osborne, 1996, no. 4), then "Who Will Save Your Soul?" (Jewel, 1996, no. 11). But heck, believing in God is mostly for intellectuals, who go "On & On" (Erykah Badu, 1997, no. 12). Maybe if I have a "mission," as when "Sunny Came Home" (Shawn Colvin, 1997, no. 7), even if I don't believe in transcendence, I can still be alright. Jewel sang of God's "Hands" (1999, no. 6), and Celine Dion (with R. Kelly) advised praying for strength and strong faith in "I'm Your Angel" (1998, no. 1). Two singers had publicly declared spiritual transformations during this time, and both ended up with charted hits on the subject. Madonna's "Ray of Light" (1998, no. 5) had her looking for a small part of heaven, while Alanis Morissette's sojourn to India appears in her 1998 no.17, "Thank U."

Forgiveness is a spiritual act and Ralph Breckle was able to forgive his mother after watching my performance of the "Musical History of Women."

CONTEMPLATION

After watching Dorothy's presentation, I was transformed. Throughout my whole life I had been negatively affected by my mother's anger. She had always wanted to be a doctor, but had to settle for becoming a nurse. She pushed my sisters to become doctors, but basically ignored me. But after seeing the progression of women's development in Dorothy's presentation, I now understand the source of my mother's anger and can forgive her. I've changed. I'm not sure what happened but I've discovered a confidence I once had.

Ralph G. Breckle
Dalton, Georgia

As the century drew to a close, a dream ended, too. The dream that a common girl could grow up to be a beautiful princess taken care of by her prince. Princess Diana, with her companion Dodi Fayed, was killed in an August 1997 automobile accident. Up to 2 million people lined the streets of London for her funeral, which was watched on TV by 1 billion people worldwide. The end of the dream, whose downfall had started with the breakdown of her marriage. From then we started to learn from her and from popular music that we had to be grown-ups and take responsibility for our own happiness.

By the end of the century, women showed once again that they had more "Wide Open Spaces" (Dixie Chicks, 1999, no. 1) when the U.S. women's soccer team captured international attention when they won the World Cup in 1999. Somehow it had escaped much notice that this was the second win, the first having been in 1991. Czech-born Madeline Albright, who finished her doctorate at Columbia University by studying while her three daughters slept at night, became the first female U.S. Secretary of State in 1997.

Andrea Jung became the first woman to head a large U.S. Corporation when she was appointed president of Avon Industries (cosmetics) in 1998. After a successful stint running Lucent Technologies, Carly Fiorina showed she was more than the stereotype of "Just a Girl" (No Doubt, 1996, no. 23) when she became the first CEO of a Fortune 100 company, for Hewlett-Packard, making her responsible for $50 billion yearly revenues and ninety thousand employees worldwide. Now spearheading a major overhaul, the new CEO hopes to bring the behemoth company into the twenty-first century as a superstar. Fiorina was recruited to HP and she left Lucent Technologies in the able hands of engineer-turned-CEO Deb Hopkins. Relying on her own awesome strength, resilience, and skills, role model par excellence Oprah Winfrey looked for the "Hero" (Mariah Carey, 1993, no. 1) within and became the top earner of all U.S. entertainers in 1998 at $49 million a year. Taking over as president and CEO of the successful eBay Internet auction in 1998, forty-something Harvard

MBAer Meg Whitman (formerly with Disney, Stride-Rite Shoes, and Hasbro) has been moving the billion-dollar company into larger-ticket items and buying insurance to protect buyers from fraud, as well as going global.

Most people have heard of PalmPilots, but may not know that Donna Dubinsky was the CEO that launched the PalmPilot (invented by company cofounder Paul Hawkins) in 1996 and is called the mother of the handheld computer industry. But she didn't start anywhere near the top; the Harvard grad took her first job in customer support for Apple Computers at thirty thousand a year. After selling PalmPilot to U.S. Robotics and later to 3Com, Dubinsky felt constrained in the mega-industry environment. So in 1998, she and Hawkins launched yet another handheld computer business, Handspring, which became PalmPilot's biggest competitor.

The following year—in 1999—Julia Roberts would become the first woman to earn more than the $20 million barrier in fees paid per movie. She became a part of the exclusive crowd, including Tom Cruise, Harrison Ford, Arnold Schwarzenegger, John Travolta, and Tom Hanks. Roberts had traveled a long way up.

Coming a distance is what Marsha Robichaux did in her last year of marriage, as she describes below, after attending one of my performances.

COMTEMPLATION

That is a great presentation you have put together. I went through the whole progression during the year of my divorce after twenty years of marriage. And this is someone who "thought" she was independent/equal/had it together, etc. At least I didn't do the "and he beats me," but I did allow more disrespect than I ever thought I'd put up with. I went through he's "My Man" [Fanny Brice, 1922, no. 10], "Stand by Your Man" [Tammy Wynette, 1968, no. 19], "Johnny Get Angry" [Joanie

Sommers, 1962, no. 7], and a *long* period of "The End of the World" [Skeeter Davis, 1963, no. 2]. However, now I am up to "I Will Survive" [Gloria Gaynor, 1979, no. 1] without doing too much of "These Boots Are Made for Walkin'" [Nancy Sinatra, 1966, no. 1]. Owning "You Don't Own Me," [Leslie Gore, 1964, no. 2] me was never an option or a thought. And I am well on the way to "Wide Open Spaces" [Dixie Chicks, 1999, no. 1] and "Stand Beside Me" [Jo Dee Messina, 1999, no. 34]. It has been an interesting year watching myself go through all of this.

Again, thanks for putting this together. I think it has amazing potential to educate all ages.

Marsha Robichaux,
Lafayette, Colorado

The journey of women's voice in popular music in this century has been a long one. It started with the victim Compliant, then progressed to Rebel, to Wonder Woman, then Cynic, and finally to responsible and adult Lilith with spirit.

The journey of women at work and in society has been a long one in the past hundred years. In 1900, consider that women lacked many freedoms we take for granted. They were imprisoned in uncomfortable and restrictive corsets, in order to be seen as ladies. Without the right to vote in most nations (with the exception of New Zealand, which granted that right in 1893), they were barred from participating in most professions or entering many universities. Laws restricted their ability to testify in court, or own property, and they were barred from serving on juries. For their livelihood they were almost completely dependent on the good will of some man—either a father, husband, or brother. Husbands, who owned their wives' income, could discipline and beat them without legal consequence. Even in 1923 women who married automatically lost their jobs as teachers. The U.S. Supreme Court struck down the minimum wage law for women in 1923, which meant it took a long time for women's wages to climb above their 1920's level of 57 percent of males'. By 1999 it had increased to 74 percent. In 1930 only 2 percent of women were lawyers, but in 1996, 40 percent of graduates from medical and law schools were women.

At the beginning of the century, women had almost no positions of power, with only 4 percent of management positions held by women. By 1999, that number had risen to 44.4 percent, while the number of females in top management positions rose from near zero to 6 percent in 2000. Decades ago, women were seen as unsuitable for leadership positions. They were too emotional, not rational enough, unable to handle conflict, inexperienced in being a team member from lack of sports participation. Those perceptions changed over the years, until 2000, when studies showed that women actually had better leadership skills than men.

Though women in top management are still underrepresented, there is movement, with two women (Jung and Fiorina) named as CEOs of *Fortune* 500 companies in the last few years of the century. Women now make up 12.5 percent of corporate officers in these companies. In addition, earnings of women corporate officers is increasing. Making up about 4 percent (93 of a total 2,225) of the top five *Fortune* 500 companies, women's share more than tripled from 1.2 percent in 1995. The 1,250 vice presidents and above-mentioned females in U.S. companies earn on the average $250,000 per year. And finally, women are getting appointed to corporate boards of directors, with 75 percent of *Fortune* 500 companies having at least one female. Minority women are gaining, too, as exemplified by the appointment in 2000 of Ruth J. Simmons as the first woman president of Brown University and the first African-American to be president of an Ivy League university.

In 1900, only nineteen women competed in the Olympics (1.5 percent of the athletes) in two events: tennis and golf. Compare that to the Sydney Summer Olympics in 2000, where about 4,200 women competed in 118 events. As an all-time high, 40 percent of the contenders were women. Because of the United States' unique Title IX legislation, a whole generation of American women have benefited from opportunities in athletics, resulting in the spectacular success of the U.S. ice hockey team at the 1998 Winter Olympics (gold medal) and the U.S. women's soccer team, who won the World Cup in 1991 and again in 1999, capturing the world's attention.

There are many hurdles still to overcome for women—many fights left. Female genital mutilation is still practiced in some countries. Girls are sold off for child marriages in certain places. Women were punished if they didn't wear veils in places such as Afghanistan, where the Taliban had strict and punitive rules on women's behavior. Domestic violence continues to take the lives of three thousand women per year, and three-fourths of these women are killed after they leave their partner. In fact, reports of domestic violence have actually been increasing, going up 117 percent from 1983 to 1991. And while there are 3,800 animal shelters in the United States, there are only 1,500 battered women's shelters.

The good news in the midst of those depressing statistics is that, at least, beating up a spouse is now illegal. Up until recent years, the abuser would not be arrested unless the victim pressed charges, something difficult for a woman to do when she is threatened by more violence. Now, though, in many counties in the States, police will carry out an arrest if they see evidence of abuse, whether the woman wants to press charges or not. Legally required abuser programs are growing in numbers, with results showing it is possible for batterers to change. It wasn't until the late 1970s that a woman could file a restraining order against a violent husband, unless she also filed for divorce at the same time. Criminalization of domestic violence did not really begin as a legal process until that time. Before the 1970s, police often exercised discretion, being urged to avoid arrest, and prosecutors did not actively pursue cases. Therefore, even though it looks as if domestic violence is on the increase, the only thing we know for certain is that reports of domestic violence are up. More women have courage enough to call the police, as there is more confidence than in earlier decades that they will actually get some relief.

Yet when we consider just how far we have come in the past hundred years, it is astonishing, considering the millennia of oppression previously. We went from being the property of our husbands to presidents of corporations. In other words, we went from being property to owning property to managing property.

Popular music charted these changes. From Fanny Brice's "My Man" (1922), where she accepts his battering as normal, and Ruth Etting's "Mean to Me" (1929, no. 3), which wonders why he delights in humiliating her; to Doris Day's "Bewitched" (1950) or Dinah Shore's "Doin' What Comes Naturally" (1946), which accept either ill treatment from men or that the woman should be dumb, or Doris Day's "Que Sera Sera" (1956), where she takes no personal responsibility for her own life; to Sandy Posey's declaration that if you're "Born a Woman" (1966), you must expect to be treated like dirt; to finally getting some power with Leslie Gore's "You Don't Own Me" (1964), then Nancy Sinatra's "These Boots Are Made for Walkin'" (1966), and Helen Reddy's "I Am Woman" (1972). These were followed by Gloria Gaynor's "I Will Survive" (1979) and then the cynical songs "Material Girl" (1985) by Madonna and Tina Turner's "What's Love Got to Do with It?" (1984). And finally the songs of inner strength: Donna Summer's "She Works Hard for the Money" (1983), Whitney Houston's "Greatest Love of All" (1986), Mariah Carey's "Hero" (1993), Shania Twain's "Any Man of Mine" (1995), Alanis Morissette's "You Learn" (1996), and the Dixie Chicks' 1999 hopeful tune of a young woman striking out on her own and taking risks in "Wide Open Spaces." My own daughters travel around the world in their own wide open spaces, to places I could never have imagined at their age. Even though I wanted desperately to go to Germany in high school, I never got to Europe until I moved to Prague in 1992 with my three daughters. Now they can land in almost any country and feel at home. The struggles of my grandmother, my mother, and my own have led to their brighter futures.

The road is long, as we move toward more equality. But we are moving in the right direction and the spaces are wide and open. But where do we go from here? It is not exactly the end of popular music for women. In fact, a hundred years from now, maybe someone will be writing a book about the trends in twenty-first century popular music.

Looking back at the century, it's clear that the number of categories of songs increased during that time, as well as the complexity of themes. In the 1920s, there wasn't much besides sentimental love songs and those about compliance, whether they pointed to neediness, jealousy, or victimization. By the 1990s, there were a multitude of categories—not only compliance, but also personal growth, Lilith strength, spirituality, life is good, let's have fun, and so on. And to add to the complexity, an increasing number of songs have more than one theme in them.

Another recent trend is a "branding" of certain singers or groups with a particular theme, something not seen much before. Earlier, we had Petula Clark singing songs about happiness and sorrow, the girl groups being angry and then pathetically codependent, Mariah Carey showing extreme neediness and also well-developed adult maturity. But today, some groups are specializing. Destiny's Child, for example, primarily does songs about women's independence and strength. Britney Spears's songs are sexy and provocative, Sarah McLachlan is known for her self-reflection and Alana Morissette for her tell-it-like-it-is lyrics.

The trend that troubles me the most is how sexuality is being expressed at younger and younger ages. Despite Britney Spears's protestations of her innocence, and her public virginity, she sings *sex* and she looks the part, too. My daughters don't like her. One of them said, "Look, Christina Aguilera never claimed to be anything other than a slut. But Britney says she is pure, when she doesn't act or sing like it. She's fake." Britney's baby voice and suggestive clothing make her the most recent incarnation of the Betty Boop archetype.

Codependent songs will still be around for a while. Though various newspaper articles have reported that needy songs with passive messages are on the rise, the statistics don't bear this out. This category of songs has been constant throughout the entire century, though decreasing since the sixties and seventies. Still, you can look at any current list of songs and find some that are very codependent. But to put this in historical context, just remember that songs of strength and songs that suggest that "love is good" have been out-numbering the passive ones.

In the last five years of the century, the sales of women's music finally reached the level of men's and then went beyond it. We can expect women to continue to exert at least equal power in record sales.

It's a new century and its challenges will continue to unfold. More chances to grow. Many problems to solve. But we have come so far in these one hundred years. My grandmother would be proud.

APPENDICES

APPENDIX A
ACTUAL NUMBERS AND PERCENTAGES OF WOMEN'S TOP 40 HITS, BY DECADE

Decade	Total Top 40 Hits	Total Women's Top 40 Hits	% Top 40 Hits by Women
1900s	390	19	5%
1910s	400	44	11%
1920s	400	44	11%
1930s	400	49	16%
1940s	2,068	268	13%
1950s	2,439	452	19%
1960s	2,984	428	14%
1970s	2,403	295	12%
1980s	2,183	392	18%
1990–1994	908	226	25%

APPENDIX B
DOMINANT THEMES AND PERCENTAGES IN TOP 40 SONGS OF WOMEN

Decade	Sentimental Love	Codependent	Marriage	Spirit	Fun	Hope	Sex	Other	Total Categorized
'30s	18: 38%	24: 50%		1: 2%	5: 10%			3: 8%	49
'40s	43: 45%	23: 24%	6: 6%	1: 1%	9: 10%	4: 4%		17: 18%	95
'50s	73: 40%	72: 39%	7: 4%		6: 3%		6: 3%	32: 17%	186

Decade	Sentimental Love	Codependent	Marriage	Spirit	Fun	Assertive/Anger	Betrayal	Social Issues	Dumped	Hope	Sex	Other	Total Categorized
'60s	75: 22%	88: 26%	10: 3%	7: 2%	15: 4%	25: 7%	19: 6%	5: 1%	45: 13%	31: 9%	11: 3%	10: 3%	341

Decade	Sentimental Love; Love Is Good	Codependent (Including Dumped and Betrayed.)	Cynicism*	Spirit	Fun	Angry/Assertive	Strength and Power	Love is Good and Difficult	Life Is Tough or Happy/Social Issues	Sex as Power	Self-Growth	Total Categorized
'70s	2: 1%	47: 26%			17: 9%	29: 16%			37: 20%	51: 28%		183
Early '80s	13: 9%	32: 23%	43: 31%		7: 5%	*	27: 19%		2: 2%	13: 9%		137
Late '80s	50: 29%	24: 14%	30: 17%		3: 2%	*	41: 24%		5: 3%	19: 11%		172
Early '90s	29: 19%	21: 14%	15: 10%		2: 1%	2: 1%	24: 16%	22: 15%	5: 3%	17: 12%	5: 3%	146
Late '90s	25: 14%	22: 12%	27: 15%	11: 6%	2: 1%	3: 2%	33: 18%	22: 12%	3: 2%	24: 13%	7: 4%	184

BIBLIOGRAPHY

Blackwelder, Julia Kirk. 1997. *Now Hiring: The Feminization of Work in the United States, 1900–1995*. College Station, Texas: Texas A&M University Press.

Boyer, Paul S., et al. 2000. *The Enduring Vision: A History of the American People*. Boston: Houghton Mifflin.

Bruner, Borgna. 1999. *Time Almanac 2000*. Boston: Time Inc. Home Entertainment.

Bufwack, Mary A., and Robert Oermann. 1993. *Finding Her Voice: The Saga of Women in Country Music*. New York: Crown Publishers.

Campbell, Michael. 1996. *The Beat Goes On*. New York: Schirmer Books.

Catalyst. 1998. "Women Corporate Officers and Top Earners." *The 1998 Catalyst Census of Women Corporate Officers and Top Earners of the* Fortune *500*. New York: Catalyst.

Catalyst. 2001. *The 2000 Catalyst Census of Women Corporate Officers and Top Earners of the Fortune 500*. New York: Catalyst.

Cole, Natalie. 2000. *Angel on My Shoulder*. New York: Warner Books.

Clinton, Hilary. 1999. "Women as Citizens: Vital Voices through the Century." Address given at Millennium Evening at the White House, March 15, Washington, D.C.

Davis, Angela. 1998. *Blues Legacies and Black Feminism*. New York: Pantheon.

Bibliography

Dickerson, James. 1998. *Women on Top: The Quiet Revolution That's Rocking the American Music Industry*. New York: Billboard Books.

Douglas, Susan. 1995. *Where the Girls Are*. New York: Times Books.

Drinker, Sophie. 1995. *Music and Women*. New York: The Feminist Press.

Fagan, Jeffrey. 1996. "The Criminalization of Domestic Violence: Promises and Limits." Presentation at the Conference on Criminal Justice Research and Evaluation. NIJ Research Report Series (January).

Fagan, Michael. 1995. "Animated Cartoons in the Classical Period of American Movies." UMI Dissertations Services. Austin: University of Texas Press.

Farley, Christopher John. 1997. "Galapalooza! Lilith Fair—A Traveling Festival Featuring Female Fold-Pop Stars—Is Rocking the Music World." *Time*, 21 July.

Fisher, Helen. 1999. *The First Sex: The Natural Talents of Women and How They Are Changing the World*. New York: Ballantine Books.

French, Marilyn. 1978. *The Women's Room*. New York: Jove Publications.

Freydkin, Donna. 1998. "Lilith Fair: Lovely, Lively, and Long Overdue." CNN Interactive, 29 July.

Gaar, Gillian. 1992. *She's a Rebel*. Seattle: Seal Press.

Gregory, Hugh. 1998. *A Century of Pop*. Chicago: A Capella Books.

Gribi, Gerri. 1998. The Real Annie Oakley. http://creativefolk.com.

Hennig, Margaret, and Anne Jardim. 1977. *The Managerial Woman*. Garden City, NY: Anchor/Doubleday.

Jones, Jacqueline. 1995. *Labor of Love, Labor of Sorrow: Black Women, Work, and the Family from Slavery to the Present*. New York: Vintage Books.

Keedle, Jayne. "Fair Lilith Comes to Town." 1997. *Summertimes*, Advocate-Weekly Newspapers (June).

Kessler-Harris, Alice. 1982. *Out to Work: A History of Wage-Earning Women in the United States*. New York: Oxford University Press.

Latifah, Queen. 1999. *Ladies First: Revelations of a Strong Woman*. New York: Morrow Books.

Marsh, David. 1999. *The Heart of Rock and Soul*. New York: Da Capo Press.

Middlehurst, Lester. 1998. "The Secret Adult Life I Led as a Child Star: Lester Middlehurst Talks to Petula Clark." *The Daily Mail* (UK), 1 May.

Nathan, David. 1999. *Soulful Divas*. New York: Billboard Books.

Bibliography

The New York Times. 1999. *The World Almanac and Book of Facts*. Mahway, NJ: World Almanac Books.

O'Brien, Lucy. 1996. *She-Bop*. New York: Penguin Books.

Perone, James E. 1999. *Carole King*. Westport, CT: Greenwood Press.

Raphael, Amy. 1995. *Grrrls: Viva Rock Divas*. New York: St. Martin's.

Rosin, Larry. 1995. "Programming Differences between Men and Women. Lecture presented at the Billboard Monitor Convention, October, New York City.

Sharpe, Rochelle. 2000. "As Leaders, Women Rule." *Business Week*, 20 November, 74–84.

Strom, Sharon Hartman. 1992. *Beyond the Typewriter: Gender, Class, and the Origins of Modern American Office Work, 1900–1930*. Urbana: University of Illinois Press.

"Study Places Latest Estimate of Substance Abuse Costs at $246 Billion." 1998. *Alcoholism and Drug Abuse Week*, 18 May, 6.

Suro, Robert. 1999. "Mixed Doubles." *American Demographics*, November, 56–62.

Unterberger, Richie. 1999. *Music USA: The Rough Guide*. London: Rough Guides Ltd.

Vicinus, Martha. 1985. *Independent Women: Work and Community for Single Women 1850–1920*. Chicago: University of Chicago Press.

Wallechinsky, David. 1999. *The 20th Century*. New York: Overlook Press.

Whitburn, Joel. 1986. *Pop Memories 1890–1954*. Menomonee Falls, WI: Record Research, Inc.

———. 1995. *Pop Annual 1955–1994*. Menomonee Falls, WI: Record Research, Inc.

———. 1997. *Top Pop Singles 1955–1996*. Menomonee Falls, WI: Record Research, Inc.

———. 1999. *A Century of Pop Music*. Menomonee Falls, WI: Record Research, Inc.

Whiteley, Sheila. 1997. *Sexing the Groove: Popular Music and Gender*. New York: Routledge.

Wightman, Clare. 1999. *More Than Munitions: Women, Work, and the Engineering Industries 1900–1950*. Boston: Addison-Wesley Longman.

Wilson, Barbara Foley. 1984. "Marriage's Melting Pot." *American Demographics*, July, 34–39.

SONG CREDITS

Credit Lines arranged by copyright date.

Won't You Come Home Bill Bailey
Written by Hughi Cannon.
Public domain.

My Man
Written by Albert Lucien Willemetz
and Maurice Yvain.
Music by Channing Pollack.
English lyrics by Jacques Charles.
Public domain.

I'm Nobody's Baby
by Benny Davis, Milton Ager, and
Lester Santhy.
© 1921 (renewed) EMI Feist
Catalog, Inc.
All rights reserved.
Used by permission.
Warner Bros. Publications U.S. Inc.,
Miami, FL 33014.

Aggravatin' Papa
by J. Robinson, Roy Turk, and
Addy Britt.
© 1922 Sony/ATV Tunes LLC and
EMI Mills Music (renewed). All
rights on behalf of Sony/ATV Tunes
LLC administered by Sony/ATV
Music Publishing.
All rights reserved.
Used by permission.

Down Hearted Blues
Words and Music by Lovie Austin
and Alberta Hunter.
© 1922 Universal—MCA Music
Publishing, a division of Universal
Studios, Inc. (ASCAP).
International copyright secured.
All rights reserved.

Hard Hearted Hannah (The Vamp from Savannah)

Words and Music by Jack Yellen, Milton Ager, Bob Bigelow, and Charles Bates.

© 1924 (renewed) Warner Bros. Inc. Rights for extended renewal term in the U.S. controlled by Warner Bros. Inc., Harry Ruby Music, and Edwin H. Morris & Company, a division of MPL Communications, Inc.
Canadian rights controlled by Warner Bros. Inc.
Warner Bros. Publications U.S. Inc., Miami, FL 33014.

Someone to Watch Over Me

by George Gershwin and Ira Gershwin.
© 1926 (renewed) WB Music Corp.
Warner Bros. Publications U.S. Inc., Miami, FL 33014.

Love Me or Leave Me

by Gus Kahn and Walter Donaldson.
© 1928 (renewed) WB Music Corp. Rights for extended renewal term in U.S. controlled by Gilbert Keys Music and Donaldson Publishing Company
Canadian rights controlled by WB Music Corp.
Warner Bros. Publications U.S. Inc., Miami, FL 33014.

I Wanna Be Loved By You

Lyrics by Bert Kalmar.
Music by Herbert Stothart and Harry Ruby.
© 1928 (renewed) Warner Bros. Inc. Rights for extended renewal term in the U.S. controlled by Warner Bros. Inc., Harry Ruby Music, and Edwin H. Morris & Company, a division of MPL Communications, Inc.
All rights for Harry Ruby Music administered by the Songwriter's Guild of America.
Warner Bros. Publications U.S. Inc., Miami, FL 33014.

Ten Cents A Dance

by Lorenz Hart and Richard Rodgers.
© 1930 (renewed) Warner Bros. Inc. Rights for extended renewal term in U.S. controlled by the Estate of Lorenz Hart (administered by WB Music Corp.) and the Family Trust U/W Richard Rodgers and the Family Trust U/W Dorothy F. Rodgers (administered by Williamson Music).

Love For Sale
by Cole Porter.
© 1930 (renewed) Warner Bros. Inc.
All rights reserved.
Used by permission.
Warner Bros. Publications U.S. Inc.,
Miami, FL 33014.

You're the Top
by Cole Porter.
© 1934 (renewed) Warner Bros. Inc.
All rights reserved.
Used by permission.
Warner Bros. Publications U.S. Inc.,
Miami, FL 33014.

Trust In Me
by Milton Ager, Jean Schwartz,
and Ned Wever.
© 1934 (renewed) Warner Bros. Inc.
All rights reserved.
Used by permission.
Warner Bros. Publications U.S. Inc.,
Miami, FL 33014.

My Reverie
by Larry Clinton.
© 1938 (renewed) EMI Robbins
Catalog Inc.
All rights reserved.
Used by permission.
Warner Bros. Publications U.S. Inc.,
Miami, FL 33014.

Over The Rainbow
by E. Y. Harburg and Harlod Arlen.
© 1938 (renewed) Metro-Goldwyn-
Mayer Inc.
© 1939 (renewed) EMI Feist
Catalog Inc.
All rights reserved.
Used by permission.
Warner Bros. Publications U.S. Inc.,
Miami, FL 33014.

Strange Fruit
Words and music by Lewis Allan.
© 1939 (renewed) by Music Sales
Corporation (ASCAP).
International copyright secured.
All rights reserved.
Reprinted by permission.

Bewitched
by Lorenz Hart and
Richard Rodgers.
© 1941 (renewed) Chappell & Co.
Rights for extended renewal term in
U.S. controlled by the Estate of
Lorenz Hart (administered by WB
Music Corp.) and the Family Trust
U/W Richard Rodgers and the
Family Trust U/W Dorothy F.
Rodgers (administered by
Williamson Music).
All rights reserved.
Used by permission.

Jim
Words and music by Caesar Petrillo,
Milton Samuels, and Nelson Shawn.

Blues In The Night (My Mama Don Tol Me)

by Johnny Mercer and Harold Arlen.

Pistol Packin' Mama

Words and music by Al Dexter.

Don't Fence Me In

by Cole Porter.

No More

by Bob Russell and Toots Camarata.

Personality

Words by Johnny Burke.
Music by Jimmy Van Heusen.

The Lady From 29 Psalms

Words and music by Allie Wrubel.

Diamond Are A Girl's Best Friend

Music by Julie Styne.
Words by Leo Robin.

Half As Much

Words and music by Curley Williams.

Whatever Will Be, Will Be (Que Sera, Sera)
Words and music by Jay Livingston and Ray Evans.
© 1955, 1984 Jay Livingston Music, Inc, and Universal—Northern Music Company, a division of Universal Studios (ASCAP).
International copyright secured.
All rights reserved.
Used by permission.

Whatever Lola Wants, Lola Gets
by Richard Adler and Jerry Ross.
© 1955 Frank Music Corp.
© Renewed, assigned to J & J Ross Co. and Lakshmi Puja Music Ltd.
All rights reserved.
Used by Permission.
Warner Bros. Publications U.S. Inc., Miami, FL 33014.

Born A Woman
Words and Music by Martha Sharp.
Copyright © 1956 Painted Desert Music Corp.
Copyright renewed.
International copyright secured.
All rights reserved.
Used by permission.

The Little Blue Man
by Fred Ebb and Paul Klein.
© 1958 Trio Music Company, Inc., Alley Music Corp.
All rights reserved.
Used by permission.

Bobby's Girl
Words and music by Gary Klein and Henry Hoffman.
© 1962 (renewed 1990) EMI Blackwood Music, Inc.
All rights reserved.
International copyright secured.
Used by permission.

End of the World
Music by Arthur Kent.
Words by Sylvia Dee.
© 1962 (renewed) by Music Sales Corporation (ASCAP) and Edward Proffitt Music (ASCAP).
International copyright secured.
All rights reserved.
Reprinted by permission.

You Don't Own Me
Words and music by John Madara and Dave White.
© 1963 by Merjoda Music, Inc.
Copyright renewed, assigned to Unichappell Music Inc.
International copyright secured.
All rights reserved

Sweet Talkin' Guy
Words and music by Doug Morris, Elliot Greenberg, Barbara Baer, and Robert Schwartz.
© 1966 (renewed 1994) Screen Gems-EMI Music, Inc. and Roznique Music, Inc.
All rights controlled and administered by Screen Gems-EMI

Music Inc.
All rights reserved.
International copyright secured.
Used by permission.

Society's Child (Baby I've Been Thinking)

Written by Janis Ian.
© 1966 (® renewed) Taosongs II (BMI)/Administered by Bug Music.
All rights reserved.
Used by permission.

Wishin' And Hopin'

Lyrics by Hal David.
Music by Burt Bacharach.
© 1969 (renewed) Casa David and New Hidden Valley Music.
International copyright secured.
All rights reserved.

The Greatest Love Of All

by Linda Creed and Michael Masser.
© 1977 EMI Gold Horizon Music Corp. and EMI Golden Torch Music Corp.
All rights reserved.
Used by permission.
Warner Bros. Publications U.S. Inc., Miami, FL 33014.

9 to 5

by Dolly Parton.
© 1980 Velvet Apple Music and Warner-Tamerlane Publishing Corp.
All rights reserved.
Used by permission.

Warner Bros. Publications U.S. Inc., Miami, FL 33014.

Oh Father

by Madonna Ciccone and Pat Leonard.
© 1989 WB Music Corp., Bleu Disque Music Co., Inc., Webo Girl Publishing, Inc., and Johnny Yuma Music.
All rights o/b/o Bleu Music Co., Inc. and Webo Girl Publishing, Inc. administered by WB Music Corp.
All rights reserved.
Used by permission.
Warner Bros. Publications U.S. Inc., Miami, FL 33014.

U.N.I.T.Y.

Words by Dana Owen.
© 1997 Queen Latifah Music.
Administered by Golden Rule Music Admin. Ltd.
Used by permission.

I Want To Be Wanted

Words and music by Kim Gannon, Pino Spotti, and Alberto Testa.
© 1960 Universal—On Backstreet Music, Inc. (ASCAP).
International copyright secured.
All rights reserved.

I Am Woman

Words and music by Helen Reddy and Ray Burton.
© 1971 Irving Music, Inc. on behalf

of itself and Buggerlugs Music Co. (BMI).
International copyright secured.
All rights reserved.

I Will Survive
Words and music by Frederick J. Perren and Dino Fekaris.
© 1978 Universal—PolyGram International Publishing, Inc. on behalf of itself and Perren-Vibes Music, Inc. (ASCAP).
International copyright secured.
All rights reserved.

Why Was I Born
Words and music by Jerome Kern and Oscar Hammerstein II.
© 1978 Universal—PolyGram International Publishing, Inc. (ASCAP).
International copyright secured.
All rights reserved.

Total Eclipse of the Heart
by Jim Steinman.
© 1982, 1983—Lost Boys Music. administered by Edward B. Marks Music Company for the U.S. and Canada.
Used by permission.
All rights reserved.

Girls Just Want To Have Fun
by Robert Hazard.
© 1983 Sony/ATV Tunes LLC. All rights administered by Sony/ATV

Music Publishing.
All rights reserved.
Used by permission.

Better Be Good To Me
Written by Holly Knight, Michael Chapman, and Nicky Chinn.
© 1984 BMG Songs, Inc. (ASCAP).
All rights reserved.
Used by permission.

Sisters Are Doin' It for Themselves
Written by Annie Lennox and Dave Stewart.
© 1985 BMG Music Publishing Ltd. (PRS).
All rights for the U.S. o/b/o BMG Music Publishing, Ltd. (PRS).
Administered by BMG Songs, Inc. (ASCAP).
All rights reserved.
Used by permission

I Have Nothing
by Linda Thompson and David Foster.
© 1992 Warner-Tamerlane Publishing Corp., Linda's Boys Music and One Four Three Music.
All Rights o/b/o Linda's Boys Music administered by Warner-Tamerlane Publishing Corp.
All rights reserved.
Used by permission.
Warner Bros. Publications U.S. Inc., Miami, FL 33014.

She Works Hard For The Money
Words and music by Michael
Omartian, and Donna Summer.
© 1993 Universal—MCA Music
Publishing, a division of Universal
Studios, Inc. (ASCAP).
International copyright secured.
All rights reserved.

Hero
by Walter Afanasieff and
Mariah Carey.
© 1993 WB Music Corp.,
Wallyworld Music, Sony Songs, Inc.,
and Rye Songs.
All rights o/b/o Wallyworld Music
administered by WB Music Corp.
All Rights o/b/o Sony Songs, Inc.,
and Rye Songs administered by
Sony Music Publishing.
All rights reserved.
Used by permission.
Warner Bros. Publications U.S. Inc.,
Miami, FL 33014.

You Learn
Words and music by Glen Ballard
and Alanis Morissette.
© 1995 Universal—MCA Music
Publishing, a division of Universal
Studios, Inc. on behalf of itself and
Aerostation Corp./Songs of
Universal, Inc. on behalf of itself
and Vanhurst Place Music
(ASCAP/BMI).
International copyright secured.
All rights reserved.

**Where Have All The Cowboys
Gone?**
Words and music by Paula Cole.
© 1996 by Ensign Music
Corporation and Hingface Music.
International copyright secured.
All rights reserved.

You're Easy On The Eyes
Written by Tom Shapiro, Chris
Waters, and Terri Clark.
© 1997 Sony/ATV Songs LLC,
Hamstein Cumberland Music, Chris
Waters Music, and PolyGram
International Publishing. All rights
on behalf of Sony/ATV Songs LLC
and Chris Waters Music
administered by Sony/ATV Music
Publishing.
All rights reserved.
Used by permission.
International copyright secured.

The Power Of Goodbye
Words and music by Rick Nowels
and Madonna Ciccone.
© 1998 EMI April Music Inc.,
Future Furniture Music, WB Music
Corp., and Webo Girl Publishing,
Inc.
All rights for Future Furniture
Music controlled and administered
by EMI April Music Inc.
All rights for Webo Girl Publishing,
Inc. controlled and administered by
WB Music Corp.
All rights reserved.

Half As Much
by Curley Williams
© 1951, renewed 1979 Acuff-Rose
Music, Inc.

INDEX

Index

Index